Moments of Meditation

A 31-Day Turnaround

DR. MYRON K. JAMERSON

Moments of Meditation

A 31-Day Turnaround

DR. MYRON K. JAMERSON

Cover Image: Sabrina Jamerson

Published by:
God is Real Publishing LLC
P.O. Box 2106
Harker Heights, TX 76548
469-298-9519

ISBN: 978-1-7322605-6-6

Printed in the United States by Morris Publishing®
3212 East Highway 30
Kearney, NE 68847
1-800-650-7888
www.morrispublishing.com

DEDICATION

I dedicate this book to three men who impacted my life; I am forever changed because of them.

Bishop Nate Holcomb
I am the man I am today because of you and your teachings. You made an indelible mark on my life. I love and miss you, Sir.

Manuel Jamerson
Dad, seeing how much you loved the Lord, will forever be in my heart. I promise always to make you proud that I carry your last name.

Pastor James Williams
I liken our friendship to David and Johnathan. You were my dear friend, and I will always love and cherish our memories.

TABLE OF CONTENTS

ACKNOWLEDGEMENTS

First and foremost, I would like to thank God for giving me the wisdom, guidance, and opportunity to write this 31-day devotional. Lord, I am forever grateful.

My wife, my love, my life, my best friend—I would not be the man I am today if it weren't for you. I am forever grateful for your true love and support.

My children: Kelsey, Kareem, Ashley, Yeshua, and Noah. I thank God daily for allowing me to be your father and also to father you. All of you hold a special place in my heart.

My grandbaby: Alyssia, my grand-candy. Always know that your Pop Pop loves you.

My mother: What can I say? You have always been my supporter and encourager. I love you with all of my heart. You are the best mom this side of heaven.

My godmother: Dr. Mildred Summerville, you are our Gigi. Thank you for investing in me. I look up to, love, and respect you.

My family: Time would fail to tell of each of you who have impacted my life by loving me, from a crazy boy to a mature man.

My spiritual mother: Pastor Valerie Holcomb, thank you for praying and always having an on-time word. I love you, Ma'am.

Mama Shirley: Pastor Shirley Caesar, you don't hesitate to tell me about myself. I receive your love and wisdom. Sabrina, the boys and I are forever grateful.

My Mentors: Bishop Jesse Giddens, Apostle Johnny L. Magee Jr., Elder Art Black, and Dr. William Buntyn. Thank You for never giving up on me. You loved me through the good, bad and ugly of times. I love and appreciate each of you always and forever.

Rock City Church: Wow is the only word I can think of now. You, indeed, are the best church this side of heaven.

Spiritual Sons: Pastor Antonio Mason (Rock Church, Watertown) and Pastor Corey Butler (Rock Church, Raleigh). Thank you for allowing me to be your Pastor. I promise to always be a Model, Mentor, and Motivator to you and your ministries.

Friend: Elder Tyrone Holcomb, thank you for taking on my first book. I am forever grateful for the love and support you have shown from start to finish.

INTRODUCTION

As this 31-day devotional inspires you, commit to these five D's:

- **Dedicate** to reading all 31 days consecutively. Determine not to miss a day; be loyal these next 31 days to grow closer to the Lord.

- **Discipline** enables your quality of life to increase. Be disciplined regarding your time management. Set a specific time daily to study the devotional. Stick to the time.

- **Duty** is fulfilling your obligation, carrying out your assignment, fulfilling your purpose, and accomplishing something as a team. We are all part of the body of Christ (1 Corinthians 12:12-27). So, you must do your duty by stepping out by faith to obey what God tells you without worrying about someone else's duty.

- **Develop** by saying yes to God. "Yes" means to agree, to have the same opinion. Allow means to give permission. In other words, to yield. Step back from what you think, and let

God show you His rightful authority, wisdom and power. He has and will always prepare you for your next step.

- **Delay** not! Allow the inspiration to start today.

And Jesus kept increasing in wisdom and stature, and in favor with God and men.

Luke 2:52

DAY 1

WINNER OR WHINER

Today, look in the mirror and ask yourself: "Am I a winner or a whiner?" A winner faces the situation and says, "I am going to overcome this. I will not fail. I will not give up. I will not give in. I will trust in the Lord because He is faithful. He always has been and always will be."

Your triumph is seeing God bigger than the situation. Believing that there is nothing too hard for God equals a winner. Knowing that God is fighting for you equals a winner.

David's men spoke of stoning him. Of course, David was upset. However, he encouraged himself in the Lord and found strength.

Moses sent 12 spies to explore the Promised Land. Upon the spies' return, they gave their report. Twelve men saw the same land. Yet, two men, out of the twelve spies, didn't see the land the same as the other ten spies. The ten reported: "We entered the land. And, the land is flowing with milk and honey. Here is some of its fruit." Their report of the land went well until they said, "But."

This is where everything spiraled downhill. "But" the people who live there are strong, and the cities have massive walls.

A whiner tends to doubt and speak fear, but a winner sees opportunity.

Then Caleb (one of the two spies) silenced the winners, oops, I meant, the whiners and said, "Let's go now and take possession of the land. We are well able to conquer it, we can do it, we will certainly conquer it" (Numbers 13:30).

Caleb's words should have motivated the people to stop whining. However, it didn't. The people began to be afraid, saying "We cannot fight those people! They are much stronger than we are; we saw giants, and we are like little grasshoppers to them!" (Numbers 13:33).

My friend, it's all in how you see yourself in the battle. The Voice Bible states it this way: "We should go straight in, right away, and take it over. We are surely able!" (Numbers 13:30). That's all I needed to hear. Now, I'm excited. Let's Go! Let's Do This! We are Winners!

At this very moment, you should be excited. You should feel as if you can conquer anything. Confess: "I can do all things through Christ who strengthens me." Right now, your spirit man should be saying, "I am a Winner!"

God has given you the land. Now, get up and take authority of it. Go in and possess it! Now, repeat with confidence, "I am a winner not a whiner! I will win the fight. I am ready for any giant that comes my way, this day and any other day."

Speak to and tell that mountain, "This day you must move. God is in control of this day." Jesus is victorious. So, you are victorious. Jesus overcame the grave. So, you can overcome any dead situation in life.

Hopefully, by now, you see yourself as a winner. So shout and let the devil know, "I AM A WINNER!" Sometimes it gets so good I shout again, "I AM A WINNER!" I see every situation in my life as a God opportunity. Then, God reveals Himself, strong and mighty, on my behalf.

Point blank, when you focus on winning in life, you don't have time to be a whiner. At the end of the day, it's all in how you see God and yourself.

Meditation Scriptures

> I can do all things through Christ who strengthens me.
>
> *Philippians 4:13*

> But thanks be to God, which giveth me the victory through our Lord Christ Jesus.
>
> *1 Corinthians 15:57*

> Be strong and courageous. Do not be afraid or terrified of them, for the Lord your God goes with you; he will never leave nor forsake you.
>
> *Deuteronomy 31:6*

Think On These Things

1. Am I a winner or a whiner?
2. Did today's devotion energize you? Were you challenged? Do you want to win in life?
3. Are you ready to conquer mountains today? Then, prophesy to the mountains and tell them to move.

DAY 2

AND IT FELL ON A DAY

Today, you have a choice. You can choose to live entangled with doubt, fear, and unbelief. Or, you can choose to believe you have what it takes to succeed in life.

God's desire has ever been for His children to walk around broke, busted, and disgusted. His desire has always been for His children to live the blessed life. Sometimes, a person will look at their family and say, "Mama didn't have anything. So, I won't have anything. Daddy died of cancer. So, I will die of cancer."

Some people believe in generational curses. These same people may conclude they will never accomplish or succeed at anything in life because of generational curses.

Well, I have good news, my friend. The curse is broken. The veil was rent. So, you don't have to live in bondage ever—ever—ever again. So, now, take a praise moment and shout, "Hallelujah!"

The Bible says, "For the eyes of the Lord run to and from throughout the whole earth, to show himself strong in the behalf of those whose heart is perfect toward him" (2 Chronicles 16:9).

This day, allow God to show Himself strong on your behalf by trusting Him in every area of your life. My dear friend, God specializes in impossible things. He can and will do what no other person can do. No longer be entangled with the cares of this world. Choose this day and begin to say, "And it fell on a day, my Lord healed me." Confess: "And it fell on a day; God saved me." Declare: "And it fell on a day, my marriage was restored." Proclaim: "And it fell on a day, I received a promotion on my job." Wherever you are, emphatically declare: "And it fell on a day, _____." Fill in the blank based on your circumstance. As you keep the faith, the thing you have been praying for will suddenly manifest.

Let me share this scripture to encourage you that God's promises are true: "God is not a man, that he should lie; neither the son of man, that he should repent: hath he said, and shall he not do it? or hath he spoken, and shall he not make it good?" (Number 23:19).

Knowing the previous scripture, you can't give up, give in, or throw in the towel. God's promises are prone to occur suddenly.

And it fell on a day, Joseph went from the prison to Pharaoh placing his signet ring on Joseph's finger. Joseph went from prison clothes to a fine linen robe. Joseph went from a prison collar to a gold chain around his neck. Joseph went from walking around barefooted to riding in a chariot. Joseph went from being single to married with children. In the blink of an eye, Joseph went from the pit to the palace.

Only Pharaoh held a higher position than Joseph in all the land. Joseph named his first son Manasseh, which means

"God has made me forget all my troubles and all my father's household." Joseph named his second son Ephraim and said, "It is because God has made me fruitful in the land of suffering" (Genesis 41:52).

One lady went from having an issue of blood to being made whole. Bartimaeus went from being born blind to seeing clearly. Many went from having an issue to no issue at all.

Keep the faith. Your whole life's situation can change. Your miracle only takes a moment. So, you can lift your head and say, "It fell on a day."

Meditation Scriptures

And straightway the fountain of her blood was dried up; and she felt in her body that she was healed of that plague.

Mark 5:29

And immediately he received his sight, and followed him, glorifying God: and all the people, when they saw it, gave praise unto God.

Luke 18:43

And God blessed Noah and his sons and said to them, "Be fruitful and multiply and fill the earth.

Genesis 9:1

Think On These Things

1. Do you believe God has the power to change your situation?
2. Do you believe you will receive from God soon and suddenly?
3. Will you keep the faith until God's promise manifests?

DAY 3

YOUR THOUGHTS
DETERMINE YOUR DESTNY

I've heard it said, "It's all in your mind," and I believe it. If you change how you think, you will change the words that come out of your mouth. Ultimately, you will change your life.

Oftentimes, a person's thoughts and speech gravitate to the negative. This happens naturally. However, God always desires His children to think positively.

What is the first thing you do when someone says I need to speak with you? The average person wonders, "Did I do something wrong?"

You may ask yourself a million questions. Then, after meeting with the person, you feel embarrassed to discover the situation was favorable. Then, you say to yourself, "I got all worked up and worried for nothing."

We live in a negative society. We're taught how to be negative in early childhood development. As children, we've been subjected to our parents' worries. Then there's the criticism we learn from other children in school.

Here is another example, what's the first thing most people say on Monday? OMG, it's Monday, "Why can't today be

Friday?" Am I right? How about this complaint: "I am so tired. It was such a short weekend." Does this sound familiar? Even so, it wasn't a short weekend because each day comprised twenty-four hours.

Now, Friday morning comes, and we begin celebrating because the weekend is here. Thank God It's Friday (TGIF)! But listen, the same God that created Friday created Monday.

Every day should be a day of celebrating the goodness of God. I understand when David said, "This is the day the Lord has made, we will (not we feel) rejoice and be glad in it (Psalm 118:24)." Each day is a rich and precious gift from God because His mercies are new every morning.

We must learn to find the positive in every situation and rejoice. If you change the way you think, it will give you a better outlook on life.

The Bible says, "And be not conformed to this world: but be ye transformed by the renewing of your mind, that ye may prove what is that good, and acceptable, and perfect, will of God" (Romans 12:2).

The word conformed in Greek is metamorphic. It's where we get our English word metamorphosis. A butterfly undergoes a metamorphosis. The beginning stage of a butterfly is an egg. Next comes a caterpillar. Then from the caterpillar stage to a chrysalis. Finally, the chrysalis stage morphs into the butterfly. It's a process!

During the process, the caterpillar must believe it will become a butterfly. But, just as the butterfly has a process, we also have a process. In life, we must go from seeing negatively to seeing positively.

As we Grow in Christ, we learn to exchange the world's way of thinking for God's kingdom mindset. As a result, we see all things working for our good. Even in difficult times, we see God working on our behalf.

When a person's mindset changes, their way of thinking will change. Thus, their speech will change. Eventually, their life will change for the better, forever.

Meditation Scriptures

And to be renewed in the spirit of your minds.

Ephesians 4:23

Set your minds on things that are above, not on things that are on earth.

Colossians 3:2

When the Spirit of truth comes, he will guide you into all the truth, for he will not speak on his own authority, but whatever he hears he will speak, and he will declare to you the things that are to come.

John 16:13

Think On These Things

1. Are your thoughts mostly negative or positive?
2. What do you do when negative thoughts enter your mind?
3. Today, when negative thoughts occur, speak positive affirmations.

DAY 4

DON'T GET OFF TRACK

Hey! Now is not the time to get distracted, fall by the wayside, or even think of quitting. Hey, you! Don't get off track!

Now more than ever, you must stay focused because the enemy wants nothing more than to distract you. He knows the blessings God's sending your way.

You were doing well, and one day you got distracted. Paul told the Believers in the Galatian church, "Before you were led astray, you were so faithful. Who has deceived you, so you have turned from what is right" (Galatians 5:7 TPT).

Wow! That is powerful! It's the little foxes that spoil the vine if you're careless. Remember the days when you first got saved? Your love for God was strong. Your worship for Him and your study of His Word was just as strong.

Over time, if we aren't careful, other things will become more important than spending time with God. Are you spending time with God as you used to? Are you in worship like you were when you first got saved? Let's face it, we all have gotten distracted at some point. However, a reality check will get us back on track.

God is on the move, and we should be moving with His cloud, not the crowd. When He moves, we move, just like that. If He doesn't move, we shouldn't move. A premature move could mean death (physical or spiritual).

Over the years, technology has come a long way. Nevertheless, the Department of Motor Vehicles and the Sheriff's Office warn us not to text and drive. Why? It's a distraction. Thousands of people die or have an accident yearly from texting and driving.

Texting while driving is a distraction. I bet some drivers who caused accidents said, "This will never happen to me." Yet, that one distraction cost them or the other person injuries or death. Think of all the people who would still be alive if someone had not gotten distracted.

The old saying, "keep your eyes on the road," still holds true. So, I say to you, keep your eyes on God.

Complacency will cause a person to lose sight of God and get off track. The enemy would like nothing more than to see you complacent. He is skimming silently to destroy you and your family. The Bible warns, "Be sober, be vigilant; because your adversary the devil, as a roaring lion, walketh about, seeking whom he may devour" (1 Peter 5:8).

The definition of devour is to eat up with greediness, to eat ravenously, as a beast of prey, or as a hungry man. It also conveys to destroy or consume with rapidity and violence. To destroy, to annihilate, to consume.

Jesus sounded the alarm by saying, "The thief comes to steal, kill and destroy" (John 10:10). The devil has no power or authority over the child of God. So, please don't allow him to distract you. Don't allow the devil and his demons to cause you to miss everything God has in store for you and your family.

Some say, "I can't wait to get to heaven to receive my rewards." I beg to differ and wonder, "Why not have some of heaven's rewards here on earth?" Receive everything God has for you in this life by staying on track. Stay in the positive lane. Stay humble. Stay grateful.

Meditation Scriptures

I Have fought a good fight, I have finished the race, I have kept the faith.

2 Timothy 4:7

Let your eyes look directly forward, and your gaze be straight before you.

Proverbs 4:25 ESV

Not that I have already obtained this or am already perfect, but I press on to make it my own, because Christ Jesus has made me his own. Brothers, I do not consider that I have made it my own. But one thing I do: forgetting what lies behind and straining forward to what lies ahead, I press on toward the goal for the prize of the upward call of God in Christ Jesus.

Philippians 3:12-14

Think On These Things

1. Have you allowed distractions to get you off track?
2. If so, what are they and why?
3. If you have gotten off course, what are your plans to get back on track?

DAY 5

DON'T OVERSTAY YOUR WELCOME

Don't overstay your welcome. This means exactly what it says. Sometimes a person can stay in a particular place far too long. Familiarity sets in, and they become too comfortable.

Some people build homes in places that should be temporary. But God leads and guides our lives. So, as He moves, we move—just like that.

Some people would rather stay in a situation that isn't good. They are reluctant to allow God to shake and break some things to help them grow. Three Cs' will cause you to overstay your welcome. First, there's comfort. People try to avoid discomfort.

Sometimes God guides His children in unfamiliar or uncomfortable situations to challenge them to grow. For example, Peter said to Jesus, "Lord, if that's you, bid me to come." Jesus responded with one word: "Come." Afterward, Peter left his comfort zone, defied gravity, and stepped out on the Word spoken to him. All 12 disciples could have stepped out on the word come and defy gravity. However, they were comfortable in the boat.

Comfort makes people complain because they don't like

change. I believe it saddens the heart of God to see adults acting like babies on pacifiers. Imagine the impact of a new believer, witnessing a person saved 20 years, walking around murmuring, complaining, arguing, fussing, and fighting. It's time to grow up! If a person was 18 years old and still in the sixth grade not wanting to go to the seventh grade, we would all agree that something is wrong with that person. Because of fear, that person would rather be comfortable rather than venture to a new beginning at a new school, new opportunities, new friends, new life. Comfort causes a person to remain in a certain place versus taking the leap of faith and trusting God.

The second way to overstay your welcome is through control. Instead of wanting control, give God control. Humble yourself under His mighty hand. Thus, if we fail to humble ourselves, God will humiliate us. I don't know about you but I have been humiliated several times, because I wanted to be in control. Thus the Word of God says, "Many plans are in a man's mind, But it is the Lord's purpose for him that will stand (be carried out)" (Proverbs 19:21 AMP).

Control is a form of pride. Pride snared the devil. We are not in control of our lives; God is. So, don't spend your entire life fighting for control and miss the move of God.

Cowardness is the third way to overstay your welcome. Fear and tragedy can take the fight out of us. Everyone will experience tough times. However, it's not what you go through; it's how you get through what you are going through that makes the difference.

The Bible encourages: "God did not give us a spirit of timidity or cowardice (craving, crippling and fawning fear).

Instead, he has given us a spirit of power, love, and abilities that result in a calm, well-balanced mind and self-control" (2 Timothy 2:7 AMP).

We need the courage to come out of bad situations. God buried Moses and gave the children of Israel thirty days to mourn. God gave them a timeframe for grieving so the people wouldn't consider Moses a monument. God warned: "You have dwelt long enough in this mount" (Deuteronomy 1:6).

Every person has the power, authority, and ability to say, "I have lived, dwelt, abided in this place too long and today I'm coming out." Make up your mind, whatever situation this day you are facing, you will see it no more. If you don't move forward it may just destroy your life.

Repeat this confession: Lord, I give You everything that concerns me for I know it concerns You. So, today I choose to move forward. In Jesus' Name, Amen.

Meditation Scriptures

Do not cling to events of the past or dwell on what happened long ago. Watch for the new thing I am going to do. It is happening already—you can see it now! I will make a road through the wilderness and give you streams of water there.

Isaiah 43:18b-19 GNT

I will instruct you and teach you in the way you should go, I will counsel you with my eye upon you.

Psalm 32:8 ESV

The Lord said to Moses, "Why do you cry for me? Tell the people of Israel to go forward.

Exodus 14:15 ESV

Think On These Things

1. Are you moving forward, or are you at a standstill?
2. If you are at a standstill, when will you move forward?
3. What's stopping you from moving forward?
4. Are you focusing on your future or living in your past?
5. Encourage someone who may be overstaying a welcome situation.

DAY 6

Don't Even Think About Quitting

Have you ever wanted to give up? Nevertheless, something inside you said, "Don't quit. Don't give up." God loves us so much. He gave us His Holy Spirit to dwell on the inside of us. The Holy Spirit renders encouragement and strength when we need it.

When I want to quit, I just can't. The Holy Spirit reminds me that I've come too far, been through too much, and overcame too many things. Therefore, I can't just throw in the towel.

We had a lady, who was challenged with multiple sclerosis, in our church. By faith, we believed God for her healing. One day she fell while home alone. Feeling helpless, she began to cry, "I'm going to die. I don't want to die but no one is here to help me."

Have you ever had one of those moments? Momentarily depressed, she heard the voice of the Lord say, "Girl, get up. I'm not done with you yet. Your purpose has not been fulfilled. There is much more work for the kingdom that has to be done."

Amazingly, we can fearfully surrender to the negative circumstances rather than commanding that mountain to move. Looking at the mountain situation, we begin to say, "If one more thing happens, I am going to quit."

Allow me to encourage you. Repeat after me: "Quitting is not an option." Now say as Job said, "Though he slay me, yet will I trust Him" (Job 13:15). Better yet, confess: "I will not die; instead, I will live and proclaim what the Lord has done" (Psalm 118:17 GNT).

God will never put more on us than we can bare. He gives us a promise that He will guide us through the obstacles of life. Whether you turn to the right or to the left, your ears will hear a voice behind you, saying, "This is the way; walk in it" (Isaiah 30:21).

Notice the scripture doesn't say, "There is no other way, so go ahead and quit." Although there are so many examples of men and women in the Bible who wanted to quit, they had the stuff that sticks: patience and persistence.

Jesus is the greatest example of not quitting. He endured harshness from the Garden of Gethsemane to the Cross. The whole time He had us on His mind. Crucifixion was a horrible death; however, I believe the entire way Jesus was saying, "I can't quit now. I must fulfill my purpose."

We can barely imagine the horror of that moment as God's only begotten Son took upon Himself the death and hell you and I deserved. Yet, the Bible says, "For the joy set before him (Christ) endured the cross, despising the shame" (Hebrews 12:2). God loves us that much!

Think of all the lives that would be affected if you quit now. Sometimes, we must go back and remember. I remember being in the military and getting into some trouble. I wanted to just quit. I walked around with my head hung down because of the embarrassment to God, my family, and my church.

One day in my room, God told me, "Place your hands under your chin and lift your chin up because you are a King's kid." I lifted my head and began to walk around proud. That very moment, I learned not only who I was, but Whose I was. I belong to God. Instead of quitting, I endured hardness as a good soldier and retired from the military honorably. Don't quit. Realize you have not tapped into what God has in store for you.

Meditation Scriptures

Each time he said, "No. But I am with you; that is all you need. My power shows up best in weak people." Now I am glad to boast about how weak I am; I am glad to be a living demonstration of Christ's power, instead of showing off my own power and abilities.

2 Corinthians 12:9 TLB

For you are a people holy to the LORD your God. The LORD your God has chosen you to be a people for His prized possession out of all peoples on the face of the earth.

Deuteronomy 7:6 ESV

But as for you, be strong and do not give up, for your work will be rewarded.

2 Chronicles 15:7 NIV

Think On These Things

1. What are some things that made you quit in the past?
2. What are some things that make you want to quit now?
3. What practices are you going to instill, to ensure quitting will never be an option?

DAY 7

I FORGIVE YOU

It's difficult for many people to forgive. Well, it's not as hard as we make it. "What do I mean?" you might ask. You could contest: "This person hurt me physically, mentally, and emotionally." You may complain further: "The person took advantage of me. They abused, abandoned, lied, cheated, and stole from me."

Now, you have every right to be hurt. Yet, there is no healing until you forgive. Forgiveness isn't for them; it's for you. Forgiveness has many definitions. However, I define it as the following:

- Choosing not to hold onto something that someone did to you.

- Choosing not to live in that place of hurt any longer.

- Choosing to let go of the past to move forward in the future.

Jesus gave the best example of forgiveness. While on the cross, He said, "Father, forgive them; for they know not what they do" (Luke 23:34). Jesus did not forget what happened to Him. He chose not to dwell in that place.

The same people that were fed, healed, delivered from demonic spirits, loved on, taught and encouraged were the same ones who said, "Crucify Him!" Yet, He forgave them. Some people will say, "I'm not Jesus. Jesus is Jesus, and He can do that." I'm so glad you said that.

Now, let's look at Stephen in the Book of Acts. He was an ordinary guy. While the religious people stoned him, Stephen appealed, "Lord Jesus, receive my spirit." Then, falling on his knees, he cried loudly, "Lord, do not hold this sin against them." And when he had said this, he fell asleep (Acts 7:59-60).

In the act of being stoned, Stephen thought nothing of himself but asked the Lord to forgive those who wronged him. So, we do have the power to forgive those who have wronged us. The Bible says, "I can do ALL things through Christ, who strengthens me."

Job is another man who offers an example of forgiveness. First, Job forgave the friends who wronged him. Then, he obeyed God and prayed for them. Job's forgiveness empowered heaven to work on his three friend's behalf and his own.

Job's forgiveness and obedience released the Lord to restore his losses in double proportion. "And the LORD turned the captivity of Job when he prayed for his friends: also, the LORD gave Job twice as much as he had before" (Job 42:10).

Jesus admonished, "But I tell you, love your enemies and pray for those who persecute you" (Matthew 5:44).

Again, forgiveness is not for the offender; it's for the offended. Unfortunately, some people die in unforgiveness. They lived a life of offense, unforgiveness, bitterness, hatred, and strife. Don't allow that to be you!

Today, ask the Lord to search your heart. If there is any unforgiveness there, let it go. Be free and move forward.

Meditation Scriptures

And when ye stand praying, forgive if ye have ought against any: that your Father also which is in heaven may forgive you your trespasses.

Mark 11:25

Be kind to one another, tenderhearted, forgiving one another, as God in Christ forgave you.

Ephesians 4:32 ESV

If your brother sins against you, go and tell him his fault, between you and him alone. Then, if he listens to you, you have gained your brother.

Matthew 18:15 ESV

Think On These Things

1. Who do you need to forgive, and why haven't you forgiven them yet?
2. Make this daily declaration: "God forgives me, I forgive myself, I forgive everyone else."
3. Commit to living a life of loving and forgiving your brothers and sisters.

DAY 8

IN SPITE OF... LORD, YOU DESERVE MY PRAISE

We often endure tests, trials, and tribulations brought on by the enemy. But, even still, we must settle in our hearts despite the situation, "Lord, You deserve my praise."

Psalm 149:6 says, "Let the high praises of God be in their mouths." So going through situations shouldn't stop the high praises from coming out of our mouths.

Shadrack, Meshach, and Abednego were in a fiery furnace and still gave the Lord high praise. Their praise resulted in the king looking in the furnace and saying, "I see four men in the furnace and the fourth one looks like the son of God."

Hallelujah, this king didn't know God, but in the furnace, he saw Him. Throw your hands in the air and shout, "Hallelujah!" Let the devil know it doesn't matter what he brings your way; God still deserves your praise.

Hallelujah is the highest praise given to God. What does Hallelujah mean? It's a command imperative of three parts: Halal is praise; lu is you; and Yah is short for Yaweh the LORD. So, when you say Hallelujah, you say, "Praise the LORD!"

When you praise the Lord, you call attention to His Glory. If you want to get God excited or enter His presence, begin to shout Hallelujah! Hallelujah gets so electrifying you begin to add a few high-praise words, such as, "Lord, I Bless You; I extol You; I glorify and magnify Your Holy Name." I feel the rapture coming. How about you?

The Bible records: "This people I have formed for myself; they shall shew forth my praise" (Isaiah 43:21). Praise is not only an action but an attitude. If you act without an attitude, you are like a voice in the Grand Canyon with an echo.

You can go through the motions but not have an attitude of gratitude. Wow, that's powerful; going through the motions and nothing is happening. Instead, your praise should move the heart of God. Through praise, you thank Him for what He has done, is doing now, and will do.

Surprisingly, many people aren't grateful for anything the Lord has done for them. A good parent does everything to provide for their child. However, some children feel no matter what a parent does, it's still not enough. This grieves the heart of a parent. That's the same way God thinks about His ungrateful children.

Instead of focusing on all the blessings the Lord has bestowed upon us, we find the one thing God didn't do and magnify it. No matter what, the Lord deserves our praise.

The Word of God reads: "Thou hast turned for me my mourning into dancing; thou hast put off my sackcloth and girded me with gladness" (Psalm 30:11). So, what are you sad about? What are you upset about? Get up and dance! The Lord is good, and His mercies endure forever.

Dancing is a part of praying. After you pray, go ahead, and break out in a dance. What if my prayer request needs to be answered? The Lord still deserves your praise. Let the devil see you dance before the prayer manifests. Let him know it's coming because you're walking in victory.

If you get your paycheck and it is not enough, don't mourn. Dance because my God shall supply all your needs. When the occasion causes a celebration—dance.

If today is day one. take one minute to give God glory and praise. On day two, give two minutes. On day three, three minutes. On day four, four minutes. On day five, five minutes. On day six, six minutes. On day seven, seven minutes. Now, that's an entire week with nothing but praise. So, as you praise the Lord, start shouting, "In spite of_____,You deserve my praise!"

Meditation Scriptures

Praise the Lord! Oh give thanks to the Lord, for He is good; For His lovingkindness is everlasting.
Psalm 106:1

But as for us, we will bless the Lord From this time forth and forever. Praise the Lord!
Psalm 115:18

Then I heard again what sounded like the shouting of a huge crowd, or like the waves of a hundred oceans crashing on the shore, or like the mighty rolling of great thunder, "Praise the Lord. For the Lord our God, the Almighty, reigns.
Revelation 19:6

Think On These Things

1. Do you still praise the Lord when you are going through difficult times?
2. Is your praise like an echo in the Grand Canyon, or does your praise move mountains?
3. From this day forward, embed in your heart—Lord, You deserve my praise?

DAY 9

IT'S ACCORDING TO YOUR FAITH

Some say, "Think big!" Others say, "Ask big!" Still others say, "Believe big!" But let's not omit, "Pray big!" I have heard and done it all, but nothing seemed to happen.

Sometimes, we don't receive the things for which we pray. Why? We fail to mix our prayers with faith. For example, someone ascribed the following acronym to faith: Forward Action In Trusting Him.

Faith believes in the unbelievable to receive the impossible. Most people speak faith but have more doubt, fear, and unbelief. Curiosity outweighs faith in God in their hearts.

Jesus replied to His disciples, "If you only have faith in God" (Mark 11:22 TLB). This tells us that our faith should be in Someone, not something. The Someone is none other than God.

Bishop Nate Holcomb often used this analogy: A person can say, "I have great faith." Then the person jumps on thin ice and goes through the ice. Now, they had great faith, but it was in the wrong object.

Keeping with Bishop Holcomb's analogy: A person can possess little faith. This person can step out on thick ice and discover the ice holds their weight. Suddenly, the person trusts the ice more. Eventually, the person's faith in the thick ice allows them to run, jump and even moonwalk on the ice.

The more a person trusts God, the more they know God is faithful. He can be trusted in every area of our lives. Man will eventually fail you. God will never fail you. In fact, God promises: "I will never leave nor forsake you" (Hebrews 13:5b).

Listen, "Not one word of all the promises that the Lord hath made to the house of Israel had failed; all came to pass" (Joshua 21:45). Think about it, all the Lord's promises came to pass.

Now, think of all the times God made you a promise. The promise may have been too big to fathom, so you stopped believing it. Let me share this with you: it may be too big for you, but it's not too big for God. In John 5, a certain man had an infirmity for 38 long years. Jesus asked him if he wanted to be healed? That was his moment to say, "Yes, Lord. Instead, he said, "I have no one to put me in the pool." Jesus then said, "Get up, pick up your mat, and walk." This man moved from no faith to great faith in a split second. Just have the faith to take Him at His Word. God wants us to pray big prayers to receive big blessings in our lives and other people's lives.

There was a man in the Bible whose name was Jabez. His name in Hebrew means "He makes me sorrowful." How hard must it have been to live with a name such as "He makes me sorrowful?"

Jabez could have lived his entire life accepting his name. However, I believe that Jabez said, "The devil is a liar. Though my name means He makes me sorrowful, I choose to pray a big prayer by faith, this day." Then, Jabez called on the God of Israel, saying, "Oh that thou wouldest bless me indeed, and enlarge my coast, and that thine hand might be with me, and that thou wouldest keep me from evil, that it may not grieve me!" (1 Chronicles 4:9-10). God granted his request.

God changed Jabez's situation when he prayed in faith. So, what makes us any different? God is no respecter of persons, but it's all according to our faith.

God wants us to pray big prayers. Trust He can and will provide because He is a big God.

Meditation Scriptures

Jesus said unto him, If thou canst believe, all things are possible to him that believeth.

Mark 9:23

Jesus looked at them intently and said, "Humanly speaking, it is impossible. But with God everything is possible."

Matthew 19:26 NLT

Make your tent bigger. Open your doors wide. Don't think small! Make your tent large and strong because you will grow in all directions. Your children will take over many nations and live in destroyed cities.

Isaiah 54:2-3 ERV

Think On These Things

1. Today, pray for something large enough to guarantee failure unless God steps in.
2. Great faith. Little faith. No faith. Which of the previous statements describes your faith?
3. Examine your heart today. Ask yourself, "Do I really believe God has the power to change my situation?"

DAY 10

LORD, WEATHER THE STORMS OF LIFE

Learning to trust God is one of the hardest things to do. Why? We want to know everything that involves God's plan. We are some nosey people. I threw that in for free. May I help you today? God isn't going to reveal His entire plan for your situation. So, stop asking and start trusting.

The Lord prepares us like a good teacher prepares the student for the big test. The Bible tells us to put on the full armor of God so that we can stand against the wiles of the devil (Ephesians 6:11-18). So, God prepares us for the test. Now, it's up to us whether we pass or fail.

Here's the problem: we want to know everything about the test when our focus should be on trusting God. We must understand that God is a loving, caring, and sharing Father. He loves His children and would never hurt or harm any of us.

Some of the storms we experience are consequences of choices we've made. Our flesh is selfish—drop the h, spell it backwards, and you get the word self—and filled with selfish desires. However, it does like the consequences that come along with its selfish decisions. Nevertheless, God takes the good, bad, and the ugly. He uses our experiences for other people's gain, our growth, and His glory.

Even when we don't understand, the Lord does. Therefore, I have settled in my heart these four words and they have changed my life forever: "Lord, I Trust You." The more I learn to trust Him, the more I learn to lean and depend on Him, knowing He loves me.

Wow! God, I know you deliver me out of every situation, but if not, I will still trust You. If not, I will still praise You. If not, I will still serve You. If not, I will still worship You. You have been and will always be faithful.

It's settled in my heart; God has equipped me for every test that comes my way. God will not give us a test prematurely. That would be setting us up to fail.

Many men and women in the Bible were forerunners for us. Their lives revealed we, too, can pass tests. Job never had the book of Job to encourage himself like we have the book of Job. However, he had to take and pass the test.

Imagine losing your children. Add to that sickness in your body. Top it off with your spouse telling you to curse God and die. Job's words deliver encouragement today: "Though He slay me, yet will I trust Him." Finally, God rewarded Job with a double-portion blessing because he passed the test. The Bible says, "So the Lord blessed the latter end of Job more than his beginning" (Job 42:12a).

Abraham was tested by sacrificing his son Isaac. Next, Mary was tested when the angel told her she would have a son named Jesus. Finally, Joseph was tested, trusting that Mary remained faithful when pregnant with Jesus. Jesus said to His disciples, "Let us go to the other side," but did not tell them about the storm, winds, and flood that would occur.

Maybe if He told them, they would have decided not to go. However, in the midst of it all, Jesus rested. So, when the storm came along, He spoke to it, and it obeyed Him and calmed down. Maybe there are some storms in your life that you need to find peace and rest in them. Just say, "Peace be still."

Lift your hands today and say, "Lord, I trust You." Sometimes you fall or fail a test, but that shouldn't be the end of your story. The Bible says that a just man falls seven times but gets back up again. So, when you fail the test, get up, dust yourself off, and get back in the fight. Above all, trust God.

Meditation Scriptures

Surely God is my salvation; I will trust and not be afraid. The LORD, the LORD himself, is my strength and my defense; he has become my salvation."

Isaiah 12:2 NIV

Have I not commanded you? Be strong and courageous. Do not be afraid; do not be discouraged, for the LORD your God will be with you wherever you go."

Joshua 1:9 NIV

When I am afraid, I put my trust in you. In God, whose word I praise— in God I trust and am not afraid. What can mere mortals do to me?

Psalms 56:3-4 NIV

Think On These Things

1. Do you have a hard time trusting God? If so, why?
2. Establish in your heart today; God can, God will, but if not—He is still God.
3. Breathe in. Breathe out. Now, lift your hands and say, "Lord, I trust You."

DAY 11

MY EXPECTATION IS FROM HIM

What a powerful title! Why is the title so powerful? A person can have an expectation and fail to have an expectation from God.

Some people have an expectation from their jobs, the government, family members, and other resources. However, God is nowhere in the picture. The Bible quotes: "My soul waits thou only upon God, for my expectation is from Him" (Psalm 62:5).

So, if my expectation is from Him, why am I searching? What am I searching for that He hasn't provided? When a person wants something, they usually want it now! Like the commercial JG Wentworth, they say, "Give me my money now, Lord!"

Why can't we trust God's understanding? He knows what's best for us. How often have you said, "I'll wait on you, Lord?" But when the Lord's response took too long, you took it upon yourself to take care of the situation.

I remember the excitement of purchasing a particular vehicle. Instead of waiting patiently on the Lord, I paid for it. When you go your way, you pay your fare. The bank was happy to finance me because they knew the interest rate would be extreme.

I almost paid double for the vehicle, but I wanted to be cool. Being cool comes with a price. As children of God, we must learn to wait on Him.

The Bible says, "But they that wait upon the Lord, shall renew their strength; they shall mount up on the wings of eagles; they shall run, and not be weary; they shall walk, and not faint" (Isaiah 40:31).

My friend, just because God says, "No," it doesn't mean no forever. It could be no for the moment. But, if God gave it to us prematurely, we would do more damage to ourselves and others.

I have learned during the waiting process to say, "My expectation is from Him continually." There is a right time for everything, and everything on earth will happen at the right time (Ecclesiastes 3:1). Everything has a time and season.

Joseph waited and endured patiently for 13 years before he received his promotion in Egypt. He didn't demand, "Give me my crown; I want it now!" He had to endure trials. He endured them with his expectation in the Lord. Joseph had no idea while waiting in prison, God was perfectly positing him.

You can place frozen vegetables, meat, and broth in a pan, but it won't become a stew until the proper timing. Are you still willing to wait if you haven't heard from God about a situation?

In the waiting process, keep your expectation in God. Thus, I recommend you do these three thing:

1. Pray: Don't stop praying while waiting for your prayer request to manifest. "I wait [patiently] for the Lord, my soul [expectantly] waits, And in His word do, I hope" (Psalm 130:5).

2. Trust God: Everything is in His timing, not ours. During the process of waiting, continue smiling, rejoicing and celebrating. Refuse to be bitter or have a bad attitude.

3. Grow: In every situation, good, bad, ugly and indifferent. We grow by learning to wait patiently on the Lord.

Meditation Scriptures

For God alone, O my soul, wait in silence, for my hope is from him.

Psalm 62:5 ERV

No one who hopes in you will ever be put to shame.

Psalm 25:3 NIV

But seek first the kingdom of God and his righteousness, and all these things shall be added to you.

Matthew 6:33

Think On These Things

1. Is your expectation really from the Lord? Why or Why Not?
2. How long will you wait before you take matters into your own hands?
3. What would you consider the hardest part of waiting for the Lord? Why?

DAY 12

PAST, PRESENT, AND FUTURE

Let's set the record straight up front. Everyone has a past. Now that we have settled that, we are living in our present. But we are in expectation of our future. And our future is going to be big.

We would like to forget some situations and circumstances—particularly those that caused us and others pain. So, let me share this with you: Never forget where you come from because your past has made you who you are today.

God takes the good, bad, and ugly events in your life and turns them into something beautiful and powerful. He uses them for the good of others and our own happiness and fulfillment. Remember, what the enemy means for bad, God loves us so much that He turns it around and uses it for our good.

That situation you are embarrassed to discuss is happening to someone who needs to hear your voice. God allowed it because He knew that you could handle it.

The Lord allowed the trauma to establish our testimony. Through the trauma, we became stronger and wiser. Revelation 12:11 states: "And they overcame him (the devil) by the blood of the Lamb, and by the word of their testimony; and they loved not their lives unto the death."

Never be ashamed to say, "God brought me out; The Lord delivered me; Jesus saved me; or my God protected me." Now that we have discovered it's okay to thank God for our past, let's praise Him for our present.

After you think of the Lord's goodness, thank Him for it. I have my health and strength. I am alive and well. I may not have everything I want, but my God shall supply everything I need. Thank You, Lord!

It's so easy to meditate on our lack, rather than celebrate our needs being met. There is a saying, "I complained I had no shoes, then I saw a man who had no feet to use, so I'm blessed."

Let's take it a little further: "Not only am I blessed, but I'm better than blessed. I refuse to allow anything to hinder me from giving the Lord thanks on this day." Living in the now means not focusing on the past or worrying about the future.

Matthew 6:25-34 says, "Take therefore no thought for the morrow: for the morrow shall take thought for the things of itself. Sufficient unto the day is the evil thereof." Matthew 6:33 declares: "But seek ye first the kingdom of God."

Hence, our focus and purpose: If we seek the kingdom, we won't worry about anything. We know the Lord took care of everything concerning our families and us.

Since the Lord provides for us currently, we can trust He has adequate resources for our future. The Word of God declares: "Eye hath not seen, nor ear heard, neither have entered into the heart of man, the things which God hath prepared for them that love him" (1 Corinthians 2:9).

I encourage you to say that scripture with your name where it says (for them). Then, end it with because I love Him. That's good news!

Today, choose not to live in the past but thank God for experiencing growth because of it. Enjoy today because it's a beautiful day. Thank God for your tomorrow because great things are in store. Finally, put your sunglasses on because your future is bright. See it how God sees it—a bright, sunny day with no clouds in the sky. That's something to get excited about.

Meditation Scriptures

Now that you know these things, God will bless you for doing them.

John 13:17 NLT

He chose us in him before the foundation of the world, that we should be holy and blameless before him. In love, he predestined us for adoption as sons through Christ.

Ephesians 1:4-5 ESV

And we know that God causes everything to work together for the good of those who love God and are called according to his purpose for them.

Romans 8:28 NLT

Think On These Things

1. Are you still living in your past? Is your past affecting you daily? If so, why?
2. Do you thank the Lord continually or based on the occasion?
3. Are you excited about your future, or is it the attitude that when it gets here, it gets here?

DAY 13

ARE YOU GOING TO
STEP OUT ON FAITH OR NOT?

Lao Tzu said, "A journey of a thousand miles begins with a single step." I agree. But the first step is sometimes the hardest part of the journey.

Fear, doubt, unbelief, and excuses can stop you from stepping into your destiny. Take a moment and reflect on the times you knew God was talking to you. Yet, fear gripped your heart and caused you to miss an impactful opportunity.

"But I rejoiced in the Lord greatly, that now at the last your care of me hath flourished again; wherein ye were also careful, but ye lacked opportunity" (Philippians 4:10). I can only imagine the multitude of people who failed to fulfill their purpose because of fear.

Fear of the unknown causes a person to make excuses and ultimately miss opportunities. I have a friend whom the Lord told to quit his job and begin full-time ministry. He considered the financial obligation, and fear gripped his heart. So, rather than obeying God, he continued working on his secular job.

To this day, he says, "I don't know if God will ever open that door up again. However, if He does, I'm going to step out by faith this time." He looked at things in the natural versus the spiritual—will I succeed or fail, will it work or not, and what if?

My friend, you can't follow your mind when walking by faith. What would you say if I told you there is no failure in God? In Genesis 12:1, God told Abraham, "Leave your country, your relatives, and your father's family (house) and go to the land I will show you (Canaan, the Promise Land)." Furthermore, God promised Abram blessings that remain still today.

Genesis 12:4 says, "So Abram went..." Now, what did Abram go on? He went on a promise from God. Abram could have made excuses like Moses. Let's be honest; most people habitually make excuses. Excuses follow a person from birth to the grave. These people reason: "I can't do this because of that or this and that."

When you wanted to do something; did the reasons you couldn't outnumber the reasons you could? I wanted to do this 31-Day Inspirational book for quite some time but found every excuse for not doing it. Please don't laugh, but I took almost two years to do a 31 Day Inspirational book.

Let me ask you this: what project is in your heart that you know nobody, but God, gave it to you? Have you even started? If not, what are you waiting on? Get up. Let's go.

In the book "The Little Engine That Could," the little red engine faced climbing a steep mountain. But, instead of making excuses, he repeated, "I think I can."

David didn't make excuses when he fought the giant Goliath. Instead, David courageously said, "I come to you in the name of the Lord of Hosts. This day will the LORD deliver thee into mine hand; and I will smite thee, and take thine head from thee; and I will give your carcass to the fowls of the air, and to the wild beasts of the earth; that all the earth may know that there is a God in Israel" (1 Samuel 17:45-46).

Today, encourage yourself and say, "I can do all things through Christ who strengthens me." Then, step out by faith. As you take the first step without excuses, know that provision has already been made for you. Sometimes, we say I am waiting on God, but the reality is that God is waiting on us. Are you going to keep God waiting?

Meditation Scriptures

And without faith it is impossible to please him, for whoever would draw near to God must believe that he exists and that he rewards those who seek him.

Hebrews 11:6 ESV

Fear not, for I am with you; be not dismayed, for I am your God; I will strengthen you, I will help you, I will uphold you with my righteous right hand.

Isaiah 41:10 ESV

And he believed the Lord, and he counted it to him as righteousness.

Genesis 15:6

Think On These Things

1. Do you believe God enough to step out on faith trusting Him? If not, what's stopping you from stepping out on faith?
2. What has God instructed you to do that you haven't done yet? When are you planning to start?
3. Today, write down the benefits of stepping out on faith and doing what God instructed you to do.

DAY 14

NOTHING IS
TOO HARD FOR GOD

There's a phrase that carries much power—nothing is too hard for God. God wants us to trust Him always. Successfully doing this takes knowing nothing is too hard for Him. Ephesians 1:9 ESV says it this way: "And what is this immeasurable greatness of His power toward us who believe, according to the working of His great might."

In life, we are plagued with issues such as cancer, dementia, poverty, addictions, broken marriages, griefs and so on. When the issues occur, the Holy Spirit gently whispers— that's not too hard for me.

2 Chronicles 16:9 says, "For the eyes of the LORD run to and from throughout the whole earth, to show Himself strong on behalf of those whose heart is loyal to Him..." What is it you're going through that you think is impossible? As I share this with you, share this with others: It's not too hard for God.

"Jesus looked hard at them and said, 'No chance at all if you think you can pull it off yourself. Every chance in the world if you trust God to do it'" (Matthew 19:26 MSG). God's power (signs, wonders, and miracles) is displayed throughout the Bible for the people who believe. The question is, are you a believer? Believe God for the impossible, and God will make it possible. Let me say that again: Believe God for the impossible, and God will make it possible.

When Moses feared facing Pharaoh, God asked him, "What is in your hand?" Moses replied, "It's a rod." God said, "Stretch it out." When Moses complied, his rod became the rod of God.

Moses had to believe God for every miracle. The Bible says, "The LORD said to him, 'Who gives man his mouth? Who makes him deaf or dumb? Who gives him sight or makes him blind? It is I, the LORD. Now, go! I will help you to speak, and I will tell you what to say.'" (Exodus 4:12-13).

Jesus asked His disciples, "What is it that you have?" They replied, "A lad with five barley loaves, and two small fishes." Jesus took, blessed, and broke it. Then, He gave it to feed over 5,000 during one meal. Nothing is too hard for God.

Mary told two servants, "Whatever He (Jesus) says do; do it." Jesus told the servants to fill the water pots, and they filled them to the rim. Everything God tells us to do must be done by faith.

The occasion called for wine, not water. The servants could have complained about Jesus using water pots when they needed wine. However, through obedience, the servants gave Jesus more than their water pots; they surrendered their faith. They took the pots to the guest, and it became wine by the time the water touched the Governor's lips.

Jeremiah 32:27 declares: "Behold, I am the Lord, the God of all flesh; is there anything too difficult for me?" Wow! Is there anything God can't do? If you can accomplish it on your own, it's too small.

God is waiting to hear what comes from your mouth next. So, will you trust Him or not? Believe God for a turnaround in your life. Believe God for great and mighty things. Believe the unbelievable and receive the impossible.

God specializes in the impossible things and will do what no other power can do. If you have faith the size of a mustard seed, you can say, "Mountain move," and it will move. Allow God to move those mountains by confessing: "There is nothing too hard for You, God." See that thing come to pass by releasing your faith and trusting God. Only God can do it!

Meditation Scriptures

Now unto him that is able to do exceeding abundantly above all that we ask or think, according to the power that worketh in us,

Ephesians 3:20

Ah Lord God! Behold, you have made the heavens and the earth by Your great power and by your outstretched arm! Nothing is too difficult for You,

Jeremiah 32:17 ESV

I know that thou canst do everything, and that no thought can be with holden from thee.

Job 42:2

Think On These Things

1. Do you believe God has the power to change your situation? If not, why?
2. Who's bigger: God or your situation? Why do you believe your answer?
3. Write down some impossible things God has done in your life.

DAY 15

YOUR THINKING IS STILL TOO SMALL

Have you ever said to yourself, "That's too big for me"? Maybe you've said, "It will never happen for me." Well, you're right! It won't happen if your thinking continues to stay small.

We limit God with our small-minded thinking. Can God do it? Yes, He can! Will God do it for me? Yes, He will! Does God want to do it for me? Yes, He does!

God desires His children to see things as He sees them. We accomplish this through our spiritual eyes, not our natural eyes. God's desire is not for you to walk around broke, busted, and disgusted your entire life. Instead, He wants you to live an abundant, blessed life.

Some say, "Mama didn't have anything, so I know I will be poor." Other people spout, "My aunt died of cancer; so cancer runs in my family." The devil plots, ploys, and plans to keep you in bondage with small thoughts.

"And so, dear brothers, I plead with you to give your bodies to God. Let them be a living sacrifice, holy—the kind he can accept. When you think of what he has done for you, is this too much to ask? Don't copy the behavior and customs of this world but be a new and different person with a fresh newness in all you do and think. Then you will learn from your own experience how his ways will really satisfy you" (Romans 12:1-2 TLB).

We must learn to change how we think to experience abundant life. We can find so many things to be negative or small about, but today, start thinking big.

The God we serve is not small. He plans for you to avoid getting stuck in a rut for years. Instead, God plans to increase, favor, bless, and prosper you. The Lord is ready to open new doors and seasons and release greater opportunities for you. As you change how you think and release your faith, God takes you to places you never imagined. Isn't this exciting?

One day, God told me to close my eyes and think of something big. I obeyed Him. Then He said, "Open your eyes." I opened them. Afterward, The Lord said, "You thought too small." He had me do this three times, and my thoughts were too small every time. I thought I was thinking big, but in God's eyes, I was limiting Him with small-minded thinking.

The Bible says, "Now unto him that is able to do exceedingly abundantly above all that we could ask or think, according to the power that worketh in us" (Ephesians 3:20). Speak this: "I know You are a big God and there are big things coming my way." Bishop Nate Holcomb would say, "You got to have the nerve to ask."

God will give you wisdom on how to own your home free and clear. He will also give you wisdom to help you bless someone else with the deed to a home or a title to a car. He is no respecter of person. You just just have faith to take Him at His Word. So, go out each day expecting God to do something big in your life.

"Dear, dear Corinthians, I can't tell you how much I long for you to enter this wide-open, spacious life. We didn't fence you in. The smallness you feel comes from within you. Your lives aren't small, but you're living them in a small way. I'm speaking as plainly as I can and with great affection. Open up your lives. Live openly and expansively!" (2 Corinthians 6:11-13 MSG).

From this day forward, confess: "Father, I thank You for big opportunities, big ideas, big breakthroughs, big investments, big results. Lord, help me to be a big blessing to someone else."

Meditation Scriptures

And straightway the father of the child cried out, and said with tears, Lord, I believe; help thou mine unbelief.

Mark 9:24

Ask, and it shall be given you; seek, and ye shall find; knock, and it shall be opened unto you: For every one that asketh receiveth; and he that seeketh findeth; and to him that knocketh it shall be opened.

Matthew 7:7-8

And Elisha prayed, and said, LORD, I pray thee, open his eyes, that he may see. And the LORD opened the eyes of the young man; and he saw: and, behold, the mountain was full of horses and chariots of fire round about Elisha.

2 Kings 6:17

Think On These Things

1. Think of something big that you believe God for? Now, think even BIGGER!
2. Ask God to help you with unbelief if there is any in your heart.
3. Speak big things out of your mouth today. Your confession is your possession.

DAY 16

WHAT ARE YOU WAITING ON? LET'S GO!

Abram, get up and go! Leave your country. Leave your relatives and your father's home, and travel to the land I will show you. Don't worry—I will guide you there" (Genesis 12:1 TVB). Wow! God tells Abram to get up, leave everything, and go. Afterward, God announces He will show Abram where to go. Finally, God says, "Don't worry—I will guide you."

Ask yourself what you would do if God told you to do those three things: "Go," "I will show you," and "Don't worry—I will guide you." Our natural inclination is to figure out all the details. However, our spirit man would say, "Let's do this. Let's go."

God would never tell us to do anything without already preparing the way. He strategically gives instructions. It's up to us to follow His instructions by faith. His instructions are revealed progressively. As we follow His first command obediently, He gives us the subsequent commands. This is what we call the Believer's walk of faith.

"For we walk by faith, not by sight [living our lives in a manner consistent with our confident belief in God's promises]" (2 Corinthians 5:7 AMP). Even though it's a process, we should all strive to live a faith-filled life. When

God says move, we move just like that.

Life is full of misunderstandings. Nevertheless, one thing we should always understand and remember is God loves His children. He will always do what's right for us. Have you ever told your family, "Let's go," and everyone complies, even though no one knows where they're going, except you?

The family members may still ask, "Where are we going?" "When will we get there?" "Who's going to be there?" You reply, "Trust me." Finally, after being asked a million questions and constantly saying, "Trust me," everyone relaxes and enjoys the ride. Think about it: Just relax and enjoy the ride. Just relax in life and enjoy the journey.

On the journey, you encounter fog while driving up a mountain. Then it rains, but you keep driving. Next, there's major road construction that slows you down. Suddenly, everyone gets impatient. You remind everyone of the Word of God that says, "Let patience have her perfect work, that ye may be perfect and entire, wanting nothing" (James 1:4). Finally, after driving several hours, you make it to your destination (Myrtle Beach, South Carolina). The passengers are at peace as they display excitement, gratefulness, and complete joy for the journey. Although there were challenges, you encouraged the family because you knew the route. You knew what was in store on the journey.

Likewise, God knows everything. He has a perfect plan for our lives. Sure, there are times when we undergo bad weather conditions; this is expected. Yet, we must continue to travel. Ultimately, arriving at the destination outweighs the bad conditions on the way.

God wants us to enjoy life without focusing on negative circumstances. Instead, focus on positive experiences like a day at the beach.

Fear tries to hinder us, but I declare this day, you will display the boldness to rise and walk by faith. Your faith will move mountains. Trust God. He will never leave nor forsake you. So, take the step of faith, and "Let's go!"

Meditation Scriptures

So be truly glad. There is wonderful joy ahead, even though you must endure many trials for a little while.

1 Peter 1:6 NLT

I pray that God, the source of hope, will fill you completely with joy and peace because you trust in him. Then you will overflow with confident hope through the power of the Holy Spirit.

Romans 15:13 NLT

Then you will experience God's peace, which exceeds anything we can understand. His peace will guard your hearts and minds as you live in Christ Jesus."

Philippians 4:7 NLT

Think On These Things

1. What has God told you to do that you haven't done yet? What's stopping you?
2. Think of all the people who will be blessed when you decide to step out by faith.
3. Today, pray and ask the Lord to increase your faith. Now step out of the boat of doubt. Let's go!

DAY 17

I'M WALKING IN AUTHORITY AND VICTORY

I'm walking in authority and victory! Now say aloud: "I'm walking in authority and victory!" Notice I didn't say, "I'm suffering in defeat; I'm dying of sickness; or I'm living paycheck to paycheck." I certainly didn't say, "I'm still hurting from my past." Say it proud and out loud so the devil will know that you mean business: "I'm walking in authority and victory!"

Although many unfortunate things may occur in the natural, we can experience the supernatural life of victory. Walking in authority and victory means walking by faith, not sight.

"For in it the righteousness of God is revealed from faith for faith, as it is written, 'The righteous shall live by faith'" (Romans 1:17 ESV).

When Jesus rose from the grave, He said that all power was in His hands because death, hell, and the grave were defeated. Jesus Christ is victorious. Therefore, we are victorious. Victory is not something you achieve; it's what you receive because of what Jesus did at Calvary. Jesus' death at Calvary gives us victory, and there is nothing the devil and his demons can do about it.

When someone did us wrong as a kid, we would stick our

tongues out and shout, "Nay Nay, Ne Nay Nay!" We must laugh at the enemy. He will try anything and everything to defeat us. Go ahead and settle in your heart, refusing to walk in defeat. Walk in victory. Now, hear the word of the Lord, "I have given you more power than he has. I have given you the power to crush his snakes and scorpions under your feet. Nothing will hurt you" (Luke 10:19 ERV).

Did the previous passage say that God gave us more power than the devil? Did the passage say that God gave us the power to crush the devil's snakes and scorpions? Did the passage say that nothing the devil does will hurt us? This is our moment to shout!

Take those three promises with you today. Confess them, and watch things turn around in your life. Don't confess them arrogantly. Confess them boldly. Boldness is the Greek word parphesia; it conveys the absence of fear.

Who's mad? No one is mad but the devil. Once the child of God realizes who and Whose they are, they can access the power they possess.

Walking in victory means not worrying about anything because we know God will supply all our needs. Walking in victory means knowing no matter what Satan brings our way; it will fail. No weapon formed against us will prosper. Walking in victory is knowing we don't fear darkness because the Lord is our light. Walking in victory is knowing my hands are ordained by God to prosper.

As you read today's devotional, I pray you see yourself in victory. You see yourself walking away from defeat to live a victorious life. You witness God with you in that fiery situation. You see Him with you in the lion's den. You experience His peace, knowing Jesus is in the boat with you.

"Don't worry—I am with you. Don't be afraid—I am your God. I will make you strong and help you. I will support you with my right hand that brings victory" (Isaiah 41:10 ERV).

Go back and read that scripture again. Once you reread it, meditate on it. Then get up and walk in victory.

Meditation Scriptures

For whatsoever is born of God overcometh the world: and this is the victory that overcometh the world, even our faith.

1 John 5:4

I have said these things to you, that in me you may have peace. In the world you will have tribulation. But take heart; I have overcome the world.

John 16:33 ESV

The Lord your God is going with you to help you fight against your enemies. He will help you win!
Deuteronomy 20:4 ERV

Think On These Things

1. Do you feel you are living a victorious or defeated life? Why?
2. What area/areas do you feel defeated in? After reading today's devotional, how will you overcome those defeat area(s)?
3. Write out a short victory confession and speak it daily

DAY 18

TELL THE LORD, THANK YOU

Pastor Charles Tedder always said, "Tell the Lord, Thank You." I didn't understand it then. However, I understand it now. There is nothing worse than an ungrateful person. Do you agree? I'm talking about a person that complains about everything. Nothing is ever good enough. That person complains about their job, spouse, children, house, car, food, furniture, clothes, etc.

Does it get on your nerves just thinking about ungrateful people? Did a particular person come to mind? Sometimes, we can think of another person. Albeit, God is talking to us about us. I know that's a hard pill to swallow.

We can be some of the most ungrateful people. The Father allows us to breathe His air, and we complain. Although the Father provides, protects, makes ways, and opens and closes doors, we still complain. Essentially, our complaints convey: "God, nothing You do is good enough for us." Now, that's a powerful indictment!

Although it may not be spoken verbally, it's shown in a person's actions. So, let's stop complaining and start thanking God for all the wonderful things He has done and continues to do for us.

"Rejoice always, pray continually, give thanks in all circumstances; for this is God's will for you in Christ Jesus" (1 Thessalonians 5:16-18). The first word in the aforementioned scripture is rejoice. We are taught the definition of the prefix "re" is to do it again. The meaning of the word joy is a feeling of good pleasure. Furthermore, happiness is derived from the word happenstance, which means your happiness is based upon what situation you are in at the moment. However, joy does not depend on us or our circumstances.

Apostle Nate Holcomb said, "Joy is an inside job, knowing God has amply enough supplies to take care of all my needs." So, we can rejoice knowing God repeatedly takes care of our needs. Therefore, we owe him praise and thanksgiving.

If you want to excite God, tell Him, "Thank You," first. I thank Him for my health, strength, family, home, and job. I thank Him that my microwave works—yes, my microwave works—and, oh, the vase is paid in full. It seems so simple, yet we forget about the material things He allows us to have.

We can thank God in advance. This means we know He's fixed future events to work out in our favor according to His Word. Even if you're sick at the moment, you're still alive. Hence, your pain has a purpose. So, give God praise.

1 Thessalonians 5:16-18 concludes: "Pray continually and give thanks in all situations." All situations mean ALL situations.

"The joy of the Lord is my strength" (Nehemiah 8:10). Learn to thank God for these three things. First, past blessings.

Look back over your life and begin to tell the Lord, Thank You for the good, bad, and ugly circumstances. Through it all, He was with you and never left your side. Romans 8:28 says, "And we know that all things work together for the good of them that love the Lord." So, in the midst of it all, God deserves our thanks.

Second, present blessings. Thank God for your current condition and position. Even as you are reading this daily devotional, pause and breathe, knowing someone took their last breath. Now, say, "Thank You, Lord."

Third, future blessings. You may not know what the future holds, but you know Who holds your future—God. For this reason, no matter what situation happens in your life, learn to say these two powerful words, "Thank You."

Meditation Scriptures

Give thanks in all circumstances; for this is the will of God in Christ Jesus for you.

1 Thessalonians 5:18

But thanks be to God, that you who were once slaves of sin have become obedient from the heart to the standard of teaching to which you were committed.

Romans 6:17

The Eternal is the source of my strength and the shield that guards me. When I learn to rest and truly trust Him, He sends His help. This is why my heart is singing! I open my mouth to praise Him, and thankfulness rises as a song.

Psalm 28:7 TVB

Think On These Things

1. Ask God to show you if there is any ungratefulness in your heart. If so, ask God to forgive you and tell Him, "Thank You."
2. Do an overall assessment of your heart of gratefulness today.
3. Throughout the day, write down things you are "thankful" for, and before going to bed, say a prayer incorporating them.

DAY 19

WHO TOLD YOU THAT?

Who told you that you couldn't do it? Who told you that it wasn't possible? Who told you that there is no hope? Who told you that you wouldn't be anything because of your past? Who told you God didn't love you? WHO! WHO! WHO!

My friend, we must get past listening to the who's. All day long, voices talk to us. But we have to learn to listen to the Voice of the Lord. How do we know the voice of the Lord? We know His voice by spending time with Him. "My sheep hear my voice, and I know them, and they follow me" (John 10:27).

If we don't watch ourselves, the who's will take control of our lives, and we won't even realize it. So, who are the who's? Where did they come from?

Galatians 3:1a CSB reads, "O foolish Galatians! Who has cast a spell on you." The Holman Christian Standard Bible says, "Who has hypnotized you?" The New Heart English Bible says, "Who has cunningly deceived you?"

Now, we know what God says about us. Yet, we can allow what others say to poison our lives. If God's Word says that we can do all things through Christ who strengthens us, why do we let them say, "You can't do anything right."

They will tell us, "That won't work!" So, we never trust God and step out on faith. If God's Word says that we are blessed, why do we allow Mr. or Ms. Who to curse us? The devil can't curse what God has blessed.

If we listen to the who's negativity long enough, we will begin to speak it, see it, and eventually live in negativity. Some people live out the who's negativity and become comfortable in it. They die, never fulfilling the abundant life God had for them. All their hopes and dreams are in the grave because they chose to believe what the enemy said instead of what God's Word says.

Our actions and confessions are a result of our beliefs. Our belief is a result of our thinking. Our thinking is a result of our source. There are only two sources—the devil and God. So, be careful of who you allow to speak into your life. Don't receive it if it doesn't align with the Word of God.

An experiment was done with three glasses of water for 30 days in a Science Lab. One glass of water was told, "You are great, loved," and other positive phrases. The second glass of water was told, "You are okay, alright," and other phrases in that manner. The last glass of water was told, "You will never be anything; you are dirty; you stink," and other negative comments.

After 30 days, each glass of water was examined under a microscope. The first glass glistened beautifully. The second glass of water was clear but not as clear as the first. Finally, the third glass of water was dirty as mud.

What is the point of me telling you about those three glasses of water? Be careful who you allow to speak into your life. Everyone who speaks into your life doesn't have your best interest. If it's not what or who God says I am, I won't receive it because I am made in His image and likeness. And so are you.

Meditation Scriptures

Behold, I have engraved you on the palms of my hands; your walls are continually before me.
Isaiah 49:16

For I know the plans I have for you, declares the Lord, plans for welfare and not for evil, to give you a future and a hope.
Jeremiah 29:11

They have venom like the venom of a serpent; Like a deaf cobra that stops up its ear...
Psalm 58:4

Think On These Things

1. Would you consider yourself a positive or negative person? Why?
2. When people speak negatively in your life, do you accept or reject it? Why?
3. From this day forward, don't allow anyone to speak negatively into your life.

DAY 20

RELEASE DAY IS FINALLY HERE

Have you ever released a balloon into the air? I'm sure just about every adult has done so. But once that balloon is released into the air, chances are, it's gone forever. So likewise, when we remove burdens, hurts, pain, frustration, disappointments, and other unwanted emotions to God the Father, they should be gone forever.

"Casting all your cares [all your anxieties, all your worries, and all your concerns, once and for all] on Him, for He cares about you [with deepest affection, and watches over you very carefully]" (1 Peter 5:7 AMP).

We release our concerns, trusting that God knows how to handle all our problems. There is a saying, "Good Morning, this is God. I will be handling all of your problems today." If God is handling everything, I don't need to worry about anything.

Three daily practices help us release all trouble: First, put it in God's hands. That's the easy part. You can say, "Lord, today I give You this situation. I won't worry or stress over it any longer." Once you say it, you really have to mean it.

Second, leave it in God's Hands. Okay, this is where the problem begins. We don't want to leave it in God's hands, especially if we don't fully trust Him. How many times have you said it and taken it back because the Lord moved too slow or not according to your perfect plan for your life, like you really know what's best for you? Could that be the reason some people find themselves in the mess they are in today because they thought they knew what was best for their life?

The Bible says, "They that wait upon the Lord...." Once we release it to God, it's time to wait. In the waiting, we learn patience. While we wait, He develops our character. While we wait, He molds, makes, and shapes us into someone greater. Above all, we learn to trust the Lord in the waiting.

The Bible encourages you to trust the Lord with all your heart and lean not to your own understanding but in all your ways acknowledge Him to direct your path (Proverbs 3:5). In times of uncertainty, have faith and maintain hope. God shifts things on your behalf.

Third, don't take it back by worrying about it anymore. Worry cancels the prayer. There is a saying, "If you are going to worry, don't pray. If you are going to pray, don't worry." Most of the time, people worry about things they have no control over. Worrying causes unnecessary stress. And stress causes unhealthy physical issues. And unhealthy physical issues sometimes lead to death.

The Bible says in Philippians 4:6a TLB, "Don't worry about anything; instead pray about everything." Therefore, I put it (anything causing me to worry) in God's hands. I leave it (anything hindering me from fulfilling my purpose) in God's hands. I'm not taking it (whatever I gave to God) back by worrying.

Once you practice these three principles, life becomes stress-free. I'm not implying stress no longer exists. However, you learn not to sweat the small stuff. You learn to live a life of peace.

Our Lord gave us this promise: "Peace, I leave with you (tell Him thank you), my peace I give you (receive it). I do not give to you as the world gives. Do not let your heart be troubled and do not be afraid" (John 14:27).

Meditation Scriptures

So if the Son sets you free, you will be free indeed.
John 8:36 NIV

For the law of the Spirit of life has set you free in Christ Jesus from the law of sin and death.
Romans 8:2 ESV

Live as people who are free, not using your freedom as a cover-up for evil, but living as servants of God.
1 Peter 2:16 ESV

Think On These Things

1. What situations are you refusing to let go of? Why?
2. What giant(s) are you facing today? Give them to God and allow Him to handle them.
3. This time, when you give those situations to God:

   • Put them in God's Hand.
   • Leave them in God's Hands.
   • Don't take them back by worrying.

DAY 21

PRESS, PRAY, AND PAUSE

We were taught as kids if you catch on fire to stop, drop and roll. Likewise, there's a spiritual safety procedure when Satan attacks you and your family: press, pray, and praise.

You have to press, pray, and praise to receive the promises of God. You must press, pray, and praise when circumstances aren't favorable.

This safety procedure helps when you feel alone. It's good for the days you feel like no one cares or understands what you are going through. God understands, and He cares.

Throughout the Bible, there are examples of people who pressed their way to get to Jesus. Mark 5:25-27 details a woman who had a severe health issue. She risked her life and pressed through the crowd to get to Jesus.

Would you press if you knew God had what you needed? Well, my friend, He does. He's waiting on you to press your way through. You are on the verge of receiving it! So, PRESS!

The Bible records in Mark 2 the account of a man sick with palsy. Although his health was failing, his friends worked on his behalf. As the people pressed to be with Jesus in the house, this man's friends pressed to get into the house.

The surrounding crowd made it impossible to approach Jesus the conventional way. So, his friends climbed and ripped the rooftop off the house. Then they lowered their friend to Jesus for his healing.

These friends pressed, and I believe they prayed. Nothing happens in life until you pray. Thinking has never healed a person, but healing has occurred through the prayer of faith. "Prayers offered in faith will restore them from sickness and bring them to health. The Lord will lift them up from the floor of despair; and if the sickness is due to sin, then God will forgive their sins" (James 5:15 TVB).

As they prayed, they praised. Something special happens when we praise the Lord. Our praise causes Him to shift the atmosphere.

When the three Hebrew boys were placed in a fiery furnace, they danced in the fire. Dancing stems from praise. As a result of their dancing, the atmosphere changed. Again, the three boys were placed in the furnace, but their praise provoked the Lord's presence.

The king said, "I thought we put three men in the fire, but I see four....The fourth man looks like the son of God." God promised never to leave nor forsake us. He promised to remain with us always, even until the end of the earth.

Paul and Silas, locked in jail, had a press, pray, and praise party. The party went so well that the chains that bound them fell off.

Psalm 30:11 says, "Thou hast turned for me my mourning into dancing: thou hast put off my sackcloth and girded me with gladness." Dancing is part of our victory celebration. Victory is not something achieved; it's what we receive because of Calvary.

Before your deliverance, let the devil see you dance. Then, when the occasion calls for a celebration, dance, my friend, dance. We can detect when a person's team is winning by how they behave in a triumphant manner.

Spiritually, we are part of the tribe of Judah, and Judah means praise. So, let's start praising the Lord. When a situation needs to be turned around, break out into praise. When circumstances look bleak, remember to press, pray, and praise your way into the presence of the Lord.

Meditation Scriptures

What am I to do? I will pray with my spirit, but I will pray with my mind also; I will sing praise with my spirit, but I will sing with my mind also.

1 Corinthians 14:15 ESV

Let the Word of Christ dwell in you richly in all wisdom, teaching and admonishing one another in psalms and hymns and spiritual songs, singing with grace in your hearts to the Lord.

Colossians 3:16 ESV

I press on toward the goal for the prize of the upward call of God in Christ Jesus.

Philippians 3:14 ESV

Think On These Things

1. Are you a person that presses, prays and praises?
2. Do you have mountain-moving faith friends in your life? If not, why?
3. Think about something you are currently going through. Now, break out into a press, pray and praise. Then witness God move on your behalf.

DAY 22

WHAT YOU SAY IS
WHAT YOU GET

Proverbs 18:21 in the Message Bible says, "Words kill, words give life; they're either poison or fruit—you choose." Another translation says that men have died because of their words.

Wow, backward! What a way to start this daily devotion! Do words carry that much power? Yes, they do. Have you ever said, "I'm catching a cold?" Eventually, the cold happened.

We must understand the power that words have over our lives. Everything we say, good or bad, affects our future. In other words, speak life into your situations instead of death. Our tongues can build others up, or they can tear them down. Like an unchecked fire that doubles in size every minute, we must be careful of what we say.

Proverbs 21:23 in the Passion Translation warns: "Watch your words and be careful what you say, and you'll be surprised by how few troubles you'll have." Therefore, we must choose our words wisely before speaking. Once words are released into the atmosphere, there is no turning or taking them back.

The wrong words can ruin a relationship. For example, two people can have the best relationship. Then one day, one person speaks negatively to the other in the company of family members. The person can apologize for speaking negatively. The offended person can offer forgiveness, but the damage has already been done. The offended person may still carry the weight of embarrassment. The relationship may move on, but it will not be the same. That's how powerful a person's words can be. It can ruin or change the dynamics of a lifetime relationship.

Positive words bring positive results, and negative words bring negative results. So, Job 3:25 declares, "For the thing which I greatly feared is come upon me, and that which I was afraid of is come unto me."

Again, Job said, "The thing which I greatly feared has come unto me." Now, Job must have spoken negatively for his atmosphere to change. Think about it, your words change atmospheres. Your words have just that much power. We are accustomed to saying whatever we feel at that moment, not realizing that it affects our future. So, let's use our words positively to improve our lives and others. Our confessions become our possessions.

Psalm 39:1 in the Message Bible says, "I'm determined to watch steps and tongue, so they won't land me in trouble." My broke days are over. I am blessed in the city, in the field, when I come in and go out. I am blessed to be a blessing.

Better yet, let's back it up with scripture. Philippians 4:19 says, "But my God shall supply all of your need according to His riches in Glory by Christ Jesus." Likewise, Proverbs 30:32 conveys that if we think evil; place our hand over our mouth. This is wise instruction because if we think wrong, eventually, we'll say the wrong things.

Bishop Nathanial Holcomb taught if you don't have anything nice to say or it doesn't line up with the Word of God, turn your mouth to the station KYMS (Keep Your Mouth Shut).

We must pick and choose our battles wisely. Some battles are won by speaking. Other battles are won by being still and allowing God to fight them for you. "Intelligent people choose their words carefully. Those who know what they are doing remain calm. [Silent fools seem wise. They say nothing and appear to be smart" (Proverbs 17:27-28 ERV). Because what you say is what you get, watch what you say!

Meditation Scriptures

For "Whoever desires to love life and see good days, let him keep his tongue from evil and his lips from speaking deceit; let him turn away from evil and do good; let him seek peace and pursue it.

1 Peter 3:10-11 MSG

Whoever guards his mouth preserves his life; he who opens wide his lips comes to ruin.

Proverbs 13:3 ESV

So shall my Word be that goes out from my mouth; it shall not return to me empty, but it shall accomplish that which I purpose, and shall succeed in the thing for which I sent it.

Isaiah 55:11 ESV

Bonus: You brood of vipers! How can you speak good, when you are evil? For out of the abundance of the heart the mouth speaks. The good person out of his good treasure brings forth good, and the evil person out of his evil treasure brings forth evil. I tell you, on the day of judgment people will give account for every careless word they speak.

Matthew 12:34-36 ESV

Think On These Things

1. Learn to respond, not react to situations with your words.
2. Remember, there is no turning back once your words are released.
3. Use words today to change your current atmosphere.

Bonus: Choose the words you say wisely from this day forward.

Dr. Myron K. Jamerson

DAY 23

THE LOVE OF GOD

Say this today: "God loves me." Sometimes we think our past or present sin disqualifies us from God's love. The truth is it doesn't. God loves us!

Satan wants us to believe God doesn't love us. But listen, there is nothing you did for God to love you; there's nothing you can do for God to stop loving you. God is Love!

The most well-known scripture in the Bible says, "For God so loved the world that He gave His only begotten Son that whosoever believeth in Him should not perish but have everlasting life" (John 3:16).

God doesn't love us with eros (sexual love), storgeo (family love), or philea (brotherly love). Instead, he expresses agape (unconditional love). His unconditional love is not based on our actions (Thank You, Jesus).

Christ died for us while we practiced sin. The Lord's love is so profound we could never comprehend it. "Though the mountains be shaken, and the hills be removed, yet my unfailing love for you will not be shaken nor my covenant of peace be removed" (Isaiah 54:10 NIV). This is how the Lord expresses His compassion for us.

God, the Father, offers us a covenant of peace with His love—a peace that passes all understanding and sustains us through the storms of life. His love remains as we walk through the valley of the shadow of death. God's love protects us in the fiery furnace and is present in the lion's den. Ponder, if you will, and you'll arrive at this conclusion: the Father loves me unconditionally.

"Love is patient, love is kind. It does not envy, it does not boast, it is not proud. It does not dishonor others, it is not self-seeking, it is not easily angered, it keeps no record of wrongs" (1 Corinthians 13:4-5).

There's a song that says, "Jesus went to Calvary, to save a wretch, like you and me, that's love!"

I agree with the sentiment of this song: Calvary and, subsequently, the cross weren't for Jesus. It was for you and me. Yet, Jesus' sacrifice was birthed from His love for us.

Can you imagine the agony, pain, and suffering He knew He would endure? Nevertheless, He said, "I will go." Imagine our Lord thinking: "I know they will sin; I know they will lie, cheat, and steal, but I'll go." Furthermore, "I know some will never believe in Me and others will be ashamed of Me, but still prepare me a body, I will go."

The Lord could have thought: "The humiliation I will endure. The crucifixion lay ahead, but I love them. To set humanity free; I'll pay the penalty."

Imagining my Lord's sacrifice on the cross brings to mind another song:

Moments of Meditation

The steadfast love of the Lord never ceases,
His mercies never come to an end.
They are new every morning,
New every morning;
Great is Thy faithfulness, oh Lord;
Great is Thy faithfulness.

Listen to that song today. Reflect on the goodness of the Lord and how faithful He is to you.

Isaiah 49:16 in the English Standard Version says, "I have engraved you on the palms of my hands, your walls are continually before me." The Lord has a tattoo of you in His palm. This way, He can continually embrace you with His love.

Meditation Scriptures

God made him to be sin for us, who knew no sin; that we might be made the righteousness of God in Him.

2 Corinthians 5:21 NIV

Greater love has no one than this, that someone lay down his life for his friends.

John 15:13 RSV

In this was manifested the love of God toward us, because that God sent his only begotten Son into the world, that we might live through him. Herein is love, not that we loved God, but that he loved us, and sent his Son to be the propitiation for our sins.

1 John 4:9-10

Think On These Things

1. Have you ever sat back and thought of God's Love for you?
2. Have you ever really thought about all the things Jesus endured on the cross for you?
3. Today, sit back and think of the goodness of the Father. It should make you love and appreciate the Lord more and more, second by second.

DAY 24

LOVE, LOVE, LOVE, LOVE, LOVE...

Dionne Warwick's song, "What the World Needs Now," is such an appropriate song for the times we live in today. Truly, "what the world needs now is love, sweet love. It's the only thing that there is just too little of."

Love people unconditionally. Love them without limits. Love them until they can't take it anymore. Love them so much that you smile if you hear their name(s). When you can do this, it shows a level of growth and maturity that most people will never experience.

Be real; at some point, we all have struggled with loving ourselves and others. So many people say, "I love them, but I don't like them." Huh? That makes no sense at all. If I love you, I can't help but like you.

If our loving, caring, sharing Heavenly Father can love us through our mess, why can't we love our brothers or sisters? God commands us to love no matter what! So often, a person will say, "I love you" with their mouth but not feel love in their heart.

"Beloved, let us [unselfishly] love and seek the best for one another, for love is from God; and everyone who loves [others] is born of God and knows God [through personal experience" (1 John 4:7 AMP).

Bishop Nate Holcomb taught a message that conveyed I love God, I love myself, and I love everyone else. This phrase should be embedded in your heart. Let's put love into action. Authentic love is saying something, doing something, and giving something.

If you do something for someone you dislike, it helps you dislike them less. But conversely, if you don't do something for them, you despise them more.

Let's call today "The Good Samaritan Day" as we spread the love of God. The Bible shares the following account in the book of Luke, chapter 10: A man was traveling from Jerusalem down to Jericho when he encountered robbers. He was stripped, robbed, beaten and left for dead. A priest and a Levite passed by him, and neither had the love to stop and check on him.

How many times have we walked right past someone and just ignored them? How many times did we fail to encourage someone who needed the love of Christ? How many times could we have fed someone but were too busy to lend a helping hand?

God always has a ram in the bush. The passage goes on to say that along came a Good Samaritan. He saw the wounded man and was moved with compassion. He dressed the beaten man's wounds. Then the Good Samaritan took the victim to an Inn where he could receive more treatment. Finally, the Good Samaritan paid the innkeeper for the treatment and promised to repay for an additional cost. Are we willing to love and help those who are hurting or is it all about me, myself, and I.

Again, love is saying something, doing something, and giving something. In short, love is sacrifice. "I tell you this: whenever you saw a brother or sister hungry or cold, whatever you did to the least of these, so you did to Me" (Matthew 25:40).

Today, say to yourself: "No matter what anyone has done to me; I choose to love." Let's sing this song: "What the world needs now, is love, sweet love." When we begin to love people no matter what, it helps us live long, healthy lives.

Meditation Scriptures

Hatred stirs up strife, but love covers all offenses.
Proverbs 10:12 RSV

Love does no harm to a neighbor; therefore love is the fulfillment of the law.
Romans 13:10 RSV

A new commandment I give to you, that you love one another: just as I have loved you, you also are to love one another. By this all people will know that you are my disciples, if you have love for one another.
John 13:34-35 ESV

Think On These Things

1. Is there a person you like and do not love? If so, call their name and say I love _____.
2. How would God rate, on a scale from 1 to 10, your love for your brother and sister in Christ?
3. Do something for someone you aren't fond of or know that doesn't like you.

DAY 25

GOD IS UP TO SUM-THING BIG!

God is up to Sum-Thing, and it's going to be BIG! I can't explain it; but I know it is going to blow your mind. I want to encourage you today to "Shhh!" Keep moving forward. He is working in the midst of your situation.

We must live in expectation daily, believing God will perform His Word. He is faithful. God (the Creator, the Originator) is (present tense) up (higher place or level) to (expressing or approaching) sum (the total amount, resulting from addition) thing (an object).

Now, let's put it all together. God, the Creator of heaven and earth, is shaking, shifting, moving, and rearranging things on my behalf in heavenly (higher) places. So, it is approaching my family and me suddenly. What's approaching me? Blessings. Healings. Deliverance. Peace. Jobs. Strength. Promotions. A blessed marriage. Healthy children. And so much more. Are you catching it? Can't you see it? Do you receive it? Can't you hear the rain?

The prophet Elijah said to king Ahab in 1 Kings 18:41, "Get up! Celebrate with food and drink because I hear the sound of a rainstorm coming."

God is up to Sum-Thing! My dear friend, God wants to

add to your life. The Bible records: "My child, if you truly want a long and satisfying life, never forget the things that I've taught you. Follow closely every truth that I've given you. Then you will have a full, rewarding life. Hold on to loyal love and don't let go and be faithful to all that you've been taught. Let your life be shaped by integrity, with truth written upon your heart. That's how you will find favor and understanding..." (Proverbs 3:1-4 TPT).

Begin to confess this out of your mouth all day, every day. Get ready to see blessings everywhere you look. The Scriptures reveal: "This book of the law shall not depart out of thy mouth, but thou shalt meditate therein day and night, that thou mayest observe to do according to all that is written therein: for then thou shalt make thy way prosperous, and then thou shalt have good success" (Joshua 1:8).

God has not abandoned, ignored, forsaken, taken a break, turned His back, or forgotten about you. Instead, He is behind the scenes working on Sum-Thing BIG. The same God with you on the mountaintop will be with you in the valley low.

Confess this out loud: "God is up to Sum-Thing BIG in my life." Confess it again: "God is up to Sum-Thing BIG in my life." One more time for the Holy Spirit: "God is up to Sum-Thing BIG in my life."

Allow me to share this scripture with you. Hopefully you are solitary so that when you shout, you won't scare someone.

"Yes indeed, it won't be long now." GOD's Decree. "Things are going to happen so fast your head will swim, one thing fast on the heels of the other. You won't be able to keep up. Everything will be happening at once—and everywhere you look, blessings! Blessings like wine pouring off the mountains and hills. I'll make everything right again for my people Israel (Amos 9:13-15 msg). Then it goes on further to say, They'll rebuild their ruined cities. They'll plant vineyards and drink good wine. They'll work their gardens and eat fresh vegetables. And I'll plant them, plant them on their own land. They'll never again be uprooted from the land I've given them. "God, your God, says so. Just shout, HALLELUJAH!

The Lord said: "My words leave my mouth, and they don't come back to me without results (Isaiah 55:11 ERV). "Then he said to me, 'Do not be afraid, Daniel, for from the first day that you set your heart on understanding this and on humbling yourself before your God, your words were heard, and I have come in response to your words'" (Daniel 10:12 AMP).

Be comforted, knowing, often—if not always—in our days of deepest anxiety and trouble, when it seems our prayers do not penetrate the skies and are met with no response, God is up to Sum-Thing BIG.

See it! Believe it! Receive it! And walk in it! In Jesus' Name! AMEN!

Meditation Scriptures

And Jesus looking upon them saith, With men it is impossible, but not with God: for with God all things are possible.

Mark 10:27

I am the Lord, and there is no other, besides me there is no God; I equip you, though you do not know me, that people may know, from the rising of the sun and from the west, that there is none besides me; I am the Lord, and there is no other. I form light and create darkness; I make well-being and create calamity; I am the Lord, who does all these things.

Isaiah 45:4-7

Our Lord is great. Nothing is impossible with His overwhelming power. He is loving, compassionate, and wise beyond all measure.

Psalm 147:5 TV

Think On These Things

1. Believe God daily for signs, wonders, and miracles.
2. See God moving on your situation and turning it around for you and your family NOW.
3. Tell the Lord, "Thank You." It's already done in Jesus' Name.

DAY 26

GREATNESS LIVES INSIDE OF YOU

Has anyone ever told you that Greatness resides inside of you? If not, let me share this with you today: Greatness resides inside you. Though you may not see it or have never been told, God sees it and wants to tell you today. Sometimes, with everything going on in life, it doesn't seem that way.

However, there is something in you so great waiting to be released. It's your season to push. Push that great baby out of you. Pushing the greatness out of you means trying something new or stepping out of the boat.

"Sing, O barren, thou that didst not bear; break forth into singing, and cry aloud, thou that didst not travail with child: for more are the children of the desolate than the children of the married wife, saith the LORD" (Isaiah 54:1).

It's your season of birthing. Yes, it will be uncomfortable. Yes, it won't make sense. Yes, people will ridicule you. Yet, it's all worth it in the end. It's your year to write a book, start a business, go back to school, record music, or apply for the job even though you might not be qualified for it. Just step out by faith because greatness awaits you. Don't die with God's promises unfilled inside of you. You may not see what God sees in you. But, even so, don't die full of dreams, ambitions, and visions.

The enemy wants you to die full. God desires you to fulfill His will for your life. Before dying, Jesus announced three powerful words: "It is finished." What was finished? The will of God for Jesus' life on earth.

"It is finished" derives from the Greek word Tetelestai, which comes from the verb teleo, meaning to come to an end. Jesus experienced a successful ending. However, some finalities are not successful but rather destructive.

It's great when we can come to some conclusions, such as mortgages and car notes being paid in full. I served 22 years, eight months, and two days in the US Army. My retirement was one of the greatest days of my life. After all the struggles, heartaches, deployments, and field training exercises, I retired successfully.

Greatness doesn't stop when your accomplishment is complete. Greatness begins with each new chapter. "And I will ask the Father, and He will give you another Helper (Comforter, Advocate, Intercessor, Counselor, Strengthener, Standby), to be with you forever" (John 14:16 amp). Greatness continued after Jesus' death. Therefore, Greatness must continue after we pass on.

It's difficult to fathom God's will concerning our lives. But think of the lives that will change forever when we stop making excuses and purpose to be great.

Abraham (the father of many nations) continues to touch lives long after his death. Abraham left everything he had to follow the leading of God. Afterward, the greatness inside him flourished.

"And he brought him forth abroad, and said, Look now toward heaven, and tell the stars, if thou be able to number them: and he said unto him, So shall thy seed be. (Genesis 15:5)

Are you willing to take the first step and apply for that job? Are you willing to google that business plan? Are you willing to visit the library and check out a book on crafts? Now, please don't laugh when I mention crafts. Every store has arts, crafts, and statues.

The people who laugh at you today may work for you tomorrow. So, make an impact on the world today. Step out by faith. Allow your greatness to shine. Understand that you won't fail with God.

Meditation Scriptures

For I know the plans I have for you, declares the Lord plans to prosper you and not to harm you, plans to give you a hope and a future.

Jeremiah 29:11 NIV

His Lord said unto him, Well done thou good and faithful servant: thou hast been faithful over a few things, I will make thee ruler over many things: enter thou into the joy of thy Lord.

Matthew 25:21

Beloved, I wish above all things that thou mayest prosper and be in health, even as thy soul prospereth. For I rejoiced greatly, when the brethren came and testified of the truth that is in thee, even as thou walkers in the truth. I have no greater joy than to hear that my children walk in truth.

3 John 1:2-5

Think On These Things

1. Ask God to show you the plan He has for your life.
2. Ask God to give you the boldness to step out of the boat (of comfort and convenience) to fulfill greatness.
3. Are you willing to leave everything to be great?

DAY 27

A BAD ATTITUDE

My dear friend, before you read today's devotion, don't get offended by the title. You cannot go where God wants to take you with a bad attitude. Have you ever met a pessimistic person? Me, too. It's certainly an unpleasant experience, being around this type of person.

We must stay positive and never cross over into the negative lane. Drivers know if their vehicle drifts into the median from the proper lane. Likewise, as Christians, when we hear our thoughts and words becoming negative, we immediately pause and change our thoughts and words.

Always remember that the Spirit makes a difference in every situation (Genesis 41:38). Let's consider a young man named Joseph. The Bible says that his attitude impressed the Pharaoh (king of Egypt). Another man by the name of Daniel became second in command as a result of a positive attitude. Caleb had another spirit (Numbers 14:24). Stephen was described as having an irresistible spirit (Acts 6:10).

Thus, our attitude should be so irresistible that people are drawn to us. People should desire to be in our company because we are atmosphere changers. Our appearance should brighten up the room because, sometimes, just a person's exit brightens up the room.

While being stoned to death, Stephen requested, "Father, forgive them." Talk about a good attitude during a bad moment. Stephen was an atmosphere changer.

Concerning another account, God asks Moses, "How long will this wicked assembly keep complaining about me?" The Lord continued, "They've murmured against me, their corpses will fall, and they will never enter into the promised land, except for Caleb and Joshua." As you see, God takes having a positive attitude seriously.

Three ways to stay positive and not gravitate to the negative lane are:

1) Remember your past blessings (what the Lord has done) for you and your family. Sit, reflect, and remember when the Lord brought you out of a bad situation. Think about when the Lord didn't give you what you deserved due to His grace and mercy. Sitting back and reflecting on the goodness of the Lord will bring tears to your eyes. How can a person be negative while thinking of God's grace and mercy?

2) Appreciate your current blessings (God is caring for you). You can celebrate now because you can read this devotion. Celebrate that you are still in the land of the living. Breathe in—breathe out (Thank You, Lord)—you are still here. That was someone's last breath. So,

find the positive in your current situation(s).

3) Think about your future blessings (God's promises). The Father has promised us a land filled with milk and honey. You must, therefore, stay on track. Stay focused. Don't allow the devil to distract you and become ungrateful.

Ungratefulness will lead to a bad attitude. Instead of focusing on what they do have, the person focuses on what they don't have and begins complaining. In the Bible, the elder brother who had a loving father had a bad attitude. When his younger brother, the elder brother told his father, "Lo, these many years do I serve thee, neither transgressed I at any time thy commandment: and yet thou never gavest me a kid, that I might make merry with my friends" (Luke 15:29). Did he forget the father gave him his portion of the inheritance? Did he forget he still lives in his father's house, eating his father's food, and so on. Instead of celebrating and being thankful, he decided to walk in envy, strife, and jealousy. If we don't watch ourselves, a bad attitude can happen to any of us. A bad attitude will block someone from impacting someone else's life.

Today, make it your mission to live a positive life. First, focus on all the Lord has done for you. Then, get ready to see a change in your life and those around you.

Meditation Scriptures

Let all bitterness and wrath and anger and clamor and slander be put away from you, along with all malice. Be kind to one another, tenderhearted, forgiving one another, as God in Christ forgave you.

Ephesians 4:31-32

Finally, brothers, whatever is true, whatever is honorable, whatever is just, whatever is pure, whatever is lovely, whatever is commendable, if there is any excellence, if there is anything worthy of praise, think about these things.

Philippians 4:8

Immediately Jesus knew in his spirit that this was what they were thinking in their hearts, and he said to them, "Why are you thinking these things?"

Mark 2:8 NIV

Think On These Things

1. Would your friends/family members say that you are a more positive or negative person?
2. Are most of your associates positive or negative people?
3. Can you be corrected and still have a positive attitude? If not, why?

Bonus: *If you have a bad attitude, where do you think it stems from? What is your plan to correct it?*

DAY 28

CLEAN OUT YOUR SPIRITUAL CLOSET

Today, let's deal with the heart of the matter. "The heart is hopelessly dark and deceitful, a puzzle that no one can figure out. But I God search and examine the mind. I get to the heart of the human. I get to the root of things. I treat them as they really are, now as they pretend to be" (Jeremiah 17:9-10 MSG).

This inspiration is for those who need heart surgery. The first step to cleaning the closet of your heart is renewing your mind. This is one of the biggest struggles in a person's life. Removing the accumulative garbage in our hearts and minds can be challenging. However, it's worth it in the end. Garbage in equals garbage out. So, we must feed our minds and spirit with the Word of God and not the word of the world. God's Word encourages, "You can." The world says, "You can't." God's Word reminds us, "You are more than a conqueror." The world says, "You are and will always be defeated."

The Bible reads, "And now, as I close this letter, let me say this one more thing. Fix your thoughts on what is true and good and right. Think about things that are pure and lovely, and dwell on the fine, food things in others. Think about all you can praise God for and be glad about" (Philippians 4:8 TLB).

I love this part from the previous scripture: "Think about all you can praise God for and be glad about." I don't have time to be depressed, pressed, and suppressed when I am thinking about the goodness of God in my life.

The second step to spiritually cleaning your closet is by forgiving and releasing anger and bitterness. You should have known the aforementioned would appear in the hoarder's closet. Unforgiveness and bitterness are like garbage if you don't deal with them. After a while, they begin to stink. Don't walk around stinking because you refuse to forgive. Don't walk around allowing these heavyweights to weigh you down. Let them go. Allow God to clean out your closet.

You will go down if a cinder block is bolted around your leg and thrown into the water. Now, if you possess the key to unlock the bolt and fail to do so, there's no one to blame but yourself. So likewise, in the spiritual realm, if you hide unforgiveness and bitterness in your closet, eventually, you will spiritually die.

Ephesians 4:31-32 admonishes, "Get rid of all bitterness, rage, and anger, brawling and slander, along with every form of malice. Be kind and compassionate to one another, forgiving each other, just as in Christ God forgave you."

Fred Luskin said it best: "Forgiveness is best seen as something that will bring you peace, closure, and reduce your suffering."

Learning to laugh at yourself is the third way to clean out your spiritual closet. Some people take life too seriously. Jesus wants us to enjoy, not endure, life. Learn to have fun. Learn to laugh. Learn to live free.

Psalm 126:2 says, "Our hearts are filled with laughter, and tongues with songs of joy. Then it was said among the nations, the Lord has done great things for them." The Message Bible says at the end, "We are one happy people."

The last way to clean out your spiritual closet involves having Jesus in your everyday life. God wants a relationship with us. He wants to be in every part of our lives. If you invite Jesus into every area of your life, He will cleanse you daily. Subsequently, you will experience a daily refreshing of the spirit.

"For you have rescued me from death; you have kept my feet from slipping. So now I can walk in your presence, O God, in your life-giving light" (Psalm 56:13 NLT).

Meditation Scriptures

> But the Lord said to Samuel, "Do not look at his appearance or at the height of his stature, because I have rejected him; for God sees not as man sees, for man looks at the outward appearance, but the Lord looks at the heart."
>
> *1 Samuel 16:7 NRSV*

> He delivered us from such a deadly peril, and he will deliver us. On him we have set our hope that he will deliver us again.
>
> *2 Corinthians 1:10 ESV*

> But now rid yourselves [completely] of all these things: anger, rage, malice, slander, and obscene (abusive, filthy, vulgar) language from your mouth.
>
> *Colossians 3:8 AMP*

Think On These Things

1. What's in your closet that needs to be cleaned out?
2. How long have you been hoarding it? When will you allow the Holy Spirit of God to cleanse your closet?
3. Is what you are hoarding in the closet worth holding onto? Will you allow the hoarding to kill you spiritually?

DAY 29

THE FAVOR OF GOD

It's the season for the favor of the Lord. It's the season for God's favor upon your life. Do you believe it? "Thou shalt arise, and have mercy upon Zion, for the time to favor her, yea, the set time, is come" Psalm 102:13. So, confess: "My set time is here."

There's a set time of God when rain or favor is abundant. Rain represents His power and presence. Bishop Nate Holcomb would say, "Favor gets you things money can buy. Favor gets you things money can't buy. Favor will even get you some money."

This season, you have God's power and presence in your life. So, walk in it. The door of favor has opened for you. Now, you must be bold enough to make your request.

People say, "When praises go up, the blessings come down." I say, "When praises go up, the presence of God comes down." Our praise creates a throne for God. When the presence of God fills the place, you will see signs, wonders, and miracles.

All of us possess Jesus on the inside. However, we should desire more. I want His presence inside, manifesting on the outside of my life. We must tap into His presence. God is everywhere, but His presence is not. We must release our faith for God's presence to manifest here on earth. Where there is the presence of God, there is the glory of God. Where there is God's glory, there is God's favor.

This is your time, man and woman of God. This is the moment you've been anticipating. Just like a child on Christmas morning, there is an expectation. There is excitement. Are you excited? Are you ready? It's favor time! Allow the Holy Spirit to fill you up until you overflow. God will purge from you things that aren't like Him. The Lord will fill you with His Holy Spirit.

Favor is from the Greek word charis. Charis is where we derive the word grace. So, get your faith fixed, focused, firm, and founded on God's favor released on your life. The Bible records the account of the widow woman who obeyed the man of God, and because of her obedience, her oil never ran out. Are you willing to listen to your man of God and be obedient? If so, likewise, your favor will never run out. The oil that's upon your life will never run dry. Your cupboards will never be bare. You will never lack or be broke another day in your life. Some do, some don't, some will, and some won't. It's predicated upon your faith today.

God is going to do the supernatural in your life for His glory. Favor is here! This season the Lord is releasing special assistance, special advantages, and preferential treatment for you. His blessings will come in abundance and accelerate.

God reigns His Shekinah glory on His children (His chosen and selected few). Tell yourself: "I am one of God's select few." Jabez was one of the select few. When he prayed,

"Oh, that Thou would bless me indeed," God granted his request. In essence, Jabez conveyed how he had a rough life but desired God's season of favor. Confess to God: "It's my season. It's my time for the favor of the Lord." Once you confess that, get in receiver mode.

The sun shines and heats the water. The water evaporates, moisturizing the air. This forms a cloud, and then the rain comes down. So, likewise, Jesus (the Son) shines and heats our lives. We send up praise, and spiritual clouds form. Thus, the rain (favor of God) comes down.

So, in my Bishop T.D. Jakes voice: "Get ready! Get ready! Get ready!"

Meditation Scriptures

Ask ye of the Lord rain in the time of the latter rain; so the Lord shall make bright clouds, and give them showers of rain, to everyone grass in the field.

Zechariah 10:1 KJV

Manifest your kingdom realm, and cause your every purpose to be fulfilled on earth, just as it is in heaven.

Matthew 6:10 TPT

Ask and it will be given to you; seek and you will find; knock and the door will be opened to you. For everyone who asks receives; the one who seeks finds; and to the one who knocks, the door will be opened.

Matthew 7:7-8 NIV

Think On These Things

1. See yourself walking in the favor of God.
2. Now that you see it, confess: "I'm walking in the favor of God."
3. Now that you have seen and confessed it, receive the favor of God in your life.

DAY 30

NOT TODAY, SATAN

Ilike today's devotion title. It should be confessed out of the mouths of believers daily. Not today, Satan! Many times, we allow the enemy to mess up our entire day. Sometimes, the devil devastates through telephone calls, family members, doctor's reports, co-workers, and so on.

However, establish in your mind that you will not allow the enemy to ruin your day. In Psalms 118:24, David said, "This is the Lord's Day; I will rejoice and be glad in it." If you believe this is the Lord's Day, why would you allow the enemy to ruin it?

You have the choice of how your day will go. Again, you have the choice of how your day will go. It doesn't matter what the enemy brings your way. Continually confess the Word of the Lord. Like a lion trainer, keep cracking the whip in the night, just like in the light.

Confess now, "No weapon formed against me shall prosper. I am healed. My family is saved. I'm in my right mind." Be bold enough to confess this: "Bring it on devil because I will not allow you to steal my joy, peace, family or anything else God has given to me. I won't allow you to make me believe any different from what the Word of God says about today."

Studying the Word of God is so essential. Subsequently, when Satan comes to steal, kill, and destroy, you can say, "According to God's Word, get thee behind me, Satan." After fasting for 40 days, the devil tempted Jesus three times. With every temptation, Jesus announced, "It is written!"

The Message Bible says in Luke 4:13, "The devil retreated temporarily, lying in wait for another opportunity." After you cast that dumb devil out, know he will return to tempt, test, or try and mess up your day. "Let them shout for joy and be glad that favor my righteous cause; yea, let them say continually, 'Let the Lord be magnified who hath pleasure in the prosperity of His servant'" (Psalm 35:27 NKJV).

The Message Bible says, "I'll tell the world how great and good you are, I'll shout hallelujah all day every day" (Psalm 35:28 msg). How can we have a bad day shouting Hallelujah all day? When we allow things to bother us, we can react in the flesh and not respond with our spirit. Our spirit man says, "Shhh," Our flesh says whatever it feels in that moment.

When you find yourself upset, remember the popular question: What Would Jesus Do (WWJD)? The devil can't hit a moving target. So, keep moving forward. When you stop allowing the devil to control your day, you will see changes in your daily life.

I am not saying that your life will be perfect, and you won't have rough days. However, during rough days, trust God the most. Remember when God showed Himself strong on your behalf during the rough days?

Don't let the enemy deprive you of God's blessing. God

is faithful. God wants to bless you beyond your wildest imagination. Why? You are a child of God and joint heir with Christ. Furthermore, you are the temple of the Lord. You are a child of light.

Therefore, don't allow the devil to steal your day. Don't allow the enemy to keep you bound. Never let the devil kill your dreams, visions, or purpose.

From this day forward, declare and decree: "Every day will be a good day for my family and me. In Jesus' Name. Amen!"

Meditation Scriptures

Put on the full armor of God, so that you can take your stand against the devil's schemes.

Ephesians 6:11 NIV

For our struggle is not against flesh and blood, but against the rulers, against the authorities, against the power of this dark world and against the spiritual forces of evil in the heavenly realms.

Ephesians 6:12 NIV

Therefore put on the full armor of God, so that when the day of evil comes, you may be able to stand your ground, and after you have done everything, to stand.

Ephesians 6:13 NIV

Bonus: So let God work His will in you. Yell a loud no to the devil and watch him make himself scarce. Say a quiet yes to God and he'll be there in no time.

James 4:7-10 MSG

Think On These Things

1. Trust God to make a way of escape when the squeeze is on in life.
2. What situation(s) do you need to cast the devil out of in your life?
3. Don't allow the devil to control your life any longer. Tell him, "Get thee behind me satan, for it is written."

DAY 31

IT'S TIME TO
BELIEVE GOD AGAIN

When was the last time you believed God for something? Have you stopped believing? Have you become an unbelieving believer? Have you changed the words that were coming out of your mouth at one point? Are you doubting God's Word now? Are you wavering? Are you all over the place? If you answered, "Yes," to any or all of these questions, I want to encourage you today to start believing God again.

Forever Jones sings a song entitled, "Time to Believe." It says, "It's time to believe in what God said; it's to believe in what He promised. We see small; He sees great. When we speak doubt, He speaks faith. So, it's time to believe in what He said." Allow those words to sink in for the moment (selah).

Ask yourself: "How do I see things today? How do I see the situation(s)? How do I see dreams and visions?" We have to start seeing and believing things as God sees. We can believe. Yet, when the circumstances change, our belief system changes.

Just because the answer has not arrived, it doesn't mean it's not on the way. God will give you a promise before the miracle. Just as the angel of the Lord said to Daniel, "Do not be afraid, Daniel. Since the first day that you set your mind to gain understanding and to be humble yourself before your God, your words were heard, and I have come in response to them" (Daniel 10:12).

A troubled man named Jairus said to Jesus, "If you come to my house, I know you can heal my daughter." On the way to the miracle, the man's associates told him not to trouble Jesus any longer because his daughter had died. Jesus (knowing the next words that would come out of Jairus' mouth) told him, "Don't doubt, only believe." Mark 5:36 (nlt) says, "Don't be afraid; just have faith." The Amplified translation reads, "Only keep believing in Me and my power."

I remember a time I stopped believing. I experienced faith-failure because it felt my prayers weren't being answered. It felt like God didn't care. Have you ever felt that way? Thank God! He didn't give up on us but loved us through all our feelings.

We have to continue believing in God, especially in times of uncertainty. Understand, in the quiet times, God is still working things out on our behalf. So, keep Believing!

What has God promised you? Well, His Word is true. We just need to believe. Hebrews 6:13-18a in the Message Bible says, "When God made his promise to Abraham, he backed it all the way, putting his own reputation on the line. He said, "I promise that I'll bless you with everything I have—bless and bless and bless!' So, Abraham stuck it out and got everything that was promised to him."

Abraham believed in God. Abram believed the Lord, and the

Lord considered his response of faith as proof of genuine loyalty. And he believed the Lord, and the Lord reckoned it to him" (Genesis 15:6). "When God wanted to guarantee his promises, he gave his word, a rock-solid guarantee—God can't break his word. And because his word cannot change, the promise is likewise unchangeable" (Hebrews 6:17-18a MSG). So, God cannot lie and God will not change because if He did either one of them, He would not be God.

It's time to believe again. Don't lean to your own understanding but lean on the Father. He knows best. Let go of trying to be in control. Instead, submit to the will of God. Trust in God's ability to do what only He can do. Remember, all things are possible to those who believe.

Meditation Scriptures

God is not a man, that he should lie; neither the son of man, that he should repent: hath he said, and shall he not do it? Or hath he spoken, and shall he not make it good?

Numbers 23:19

HE asked me, "Son of man, can these bones live?" I said, "Sovereign Lord, You alone know." Then He said to me, "Prophesy to these bones and say to them. "Dry bones, hear the Word of the Lord! This is what the sovereign Lord says to these bones: I will make breath enter you, and you will come to life.

Ezekiel 37:3-5 NIV

A double minded man is unstable in all his ways.

James 1:8

Bonus: And it shall come to pass afterward, that I will pour out my spirit upon all flesh; and your sons and your daughters shall prophesy, your old men shall dream dreams, your young men shall see visions.

Joel 2:28

Think On These Things

1. Believe again.
2. Create a vision board.
3. Speak to those dormant things and tell them to awaken.

BONUS

FOR YOUR ENCOURAGEMENT

I was substituting at a school one day. I shared with the class; I was writing a 31-Day Devotional. During that time, a young lady asked if she could write an encouraging word for the devotional. I agreed to let her submit it. And this is what she wrote:

Somedays, you may feel your world is about to crumble. But realize, you can't stay down too long. You have people who care, and you have those who don't.

Life will always get worse before it gets better. Have faith that God can pull you out. God says, "Have I not commanded you? Be strong and courageous, do not be frightened, and do not be dismayed for the Lord your God is with you wherever you go" (Joshua 1:9).

Trinity Brooks
10th Grade
Jordan Matthews High School

Dr. Myron K. Jamerson

BIOGRAPHY

Dr. Myron K. Jamerson is a preacher, author, entrepreneur, song writer, psalmist, and the founder of Rock City Church from Memphis, Tennessee. With a vision in the heart of Myron to begin a ministry where God's love could be seen and performed, The Rock Church held its first service on November 27, 2011, in the dining room of Myron's home in Fort Drum, New York, through the Holy Spirit's guidance and under His leadership. He later retired from the U.S. Army in 2014 after serving more than 22 years.

Thus, Myron's teachings aim to reveal the "love of God." It's to be understood that nothing can destroy or diminish the love God has for His people.

Myron's voice reaches "the voiceless" with a message of salvation, hope, and wholeness. He passionately shares God's transformative Word with those seeking to discover their purpose in life and launch into their destiny. His heart is to demonstrate a profound love for God and compassion for people for he understands life's difficulties because he's been there and knows how to get out.

During the pandemic in 2020, Myron, inspired by the Holy Spirit, uprooted his family from Upstate New York. Just as the LORD said unto Abram to "Get thee out of thy country, and from thy kindred, and from thy father's house, unto a land that I will shew thee" (Genesis 12:1), the Spirit directed him to North Carolina, where he currently pastors Rock City Church. Myron's life purpose is "to preach and teach until they see Jesus."

Myron is happily married to Sabrina. They have five children: Kelsey, Kareem, Ashley, Yeshua, Noah and one grandcandy, Alessia.

Moments of Meditation

Dr. Myron K. Jamerson